Cyclops Toys
Through the Years
Australia's Childhood Icon

A wonderful early example of 'getting out and under'—this youngster is tinkering with Australia's first pedal car
(Reproduced courtesy of the A.M. Australian Magazine *December 1950)*

Front Cover: *The cover of the book shows the frontispiece from the 1994 Hunter's Toyline catalogue, featuring a beautifully restored Cyclops pedal car. (Reproduced with the kind permission of Hunter's Toyline).*
Back Cover: *A wonderful 'hug' of teddy bears taking a 1940s Cyclops Motor Truck, still sporting its original paint, out for a spin. (Courtesy of Judy and Steven Curnow).*

Cyclops Toys Through the Years
Australia's Childhood Icon

MARJORY FAINGES

Kangaroo Press

John Heine founded Cyclops Toys in 1913.

ACKNOWLEDGMENTS

Without the marvellous help and assistance from the following people, who so freely passed on information, this book would never have been written. My sincere thanks for their help goes to the following:

Ken Chapman (NSW)	Shirley-Anne McKay (NSW)
Peter Christensen (Qld)	Helen & John Palmer (NSW)
Barbara Hancock (NSW)	Ross Schmidt (WA)
Gary Jones (Vic)	

Thanks also to Yaffa Publications (publishers of the *Toy and Hobby Retailer*), and especially to John Hunter of Hunter's Toyline. To the staff at Rabbit Photos, Stafford for redeveloping photographs to my instructions, to the owner of the old Regent Cycles (in Newmarket, Brisbane) who kept many of the old Cyclops catalogues from the 1950s, and to the late Arthur Gorrie—also a hoarder—who kept so many copies of the old *Toy & Hobby Retailer*, thanks to all of you. Not forgetting my husband Jim, who at all times was there as a backup, to keep me plodding on what at one stage looked almost an impossible task. Many thanks to all those who willingly shared the photographs of themselves or their children playing with Cyclops through the years.

First published in 1997 by Kangaroo Press Pty Ltd
3 Whitehall Road Kenthurst NSW 2156 Australia
P.O. Box 6125 Dural Delivery Centre NSW 2158
Printed in Hong Kong through Colorcraft Ltd

ISBN 0 86417 832 8

CONTENTS

FOREWORD

This story of Cyclops records a fascinating and important development in the Australian Toy and Nursery Industries.

The impact on the perceptual sensitivities, tastes and development of the millions of children who enjoyed the vast number of the playthings developed and produced by Cyclops over the years, would make a fascinating study.

Toymakers accept the difficult challenge of marketing price-sensitive, tough and durable products which at the same time are colourful, attractive and fun, ensuring at all times a safe play environment. Cyclops met that challenge.

As a senior executive of the Cyclops group for nearly 20 years in the period to 1973, I have thoroughly enjoyed reading this story, and it brought back many pleasant memories, of both products and people. I also learned a lot!

Marjory Fainges has completed excellent research and turned it into interesting reading.

Kenneth F. Chapman
Chairman of Toy Association
4 September 1996.

Preface—Thanks for the Memories

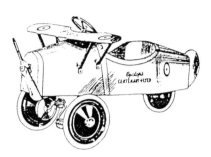

It is with great pleasure that I am able to be associated with this celebration of the first eighty years of one of Australia's greatest brands. Few products can claim such important cultural, social and historic significance, ranking with other famous Aussie icons such as Vegemite, the Victa Lawnmower, the Hills Hoist and the Southern Cross Windmill.

However, Cyclops is far more than just an icon. It has been an intrinsic part of the lives and lifestyles of millions of Australians, young and old alike, generation after generation. Australians have grown up with Cyclops as part of their own childhood, and have later been able to pass on the same enjoyment to their children and grandchildren.

Excuse the pun, but I am also somewhat 'one-eyed' about Cyclops, as I recall my own childhood and the incredible amount of fun I had over the years on my Cyclops bike and scooter. The mere mention of the name immediately brings back so many pleasant memories, with an emotional bond that only an Australian could understand.

While most of the thousands of products, representing an extraordinary diversity, presented in this book no longer exist, they can still be enjoyed as they are presented all at once for the very first time.

Like so many of our other wonderful brands, Cyclops found itself in overseas hands for many years. But I am extremely proud to have brought the ownership back home to Australia, and my family is dedicated to ensuring that many more young Australians can experience the joy of Cyclops products for many generations to come.

I salute everyone who has been involved in the compilation and production of this important publication, and I am sure that you will enjoy this unique, informative, entertaining and nostalgic trip down memory lane, as you take a voyage of discovery over eight decades.

John Hunter
Chairman of Hunter's Toyline

John Hunter, of Hunter's Toyline; bringing Australian toys to Australian children.
(Courtesy Hunter's Toyline)

INTRODUCTION

In practically every street in Australia, whether it be a tree lined suburban street, a back alley of one of our major cities, or even a dusty track in the great outback of this vast continent, there can be found an example of a child's wheeled toy that bears the name of that great Australian icon of childhood—Cyclops. It may be a little faded and worse for wear, but it still remains a much-loved item of childhood.

You only have to mention the word 'Cyclops' when a group of people are gathered together, and it is soon apparent that this word alone brings out the memories of childhood and the tremendous impact that this name has had on the children of Australia. Fond reminiscences emerge of what may have been a well-loved and battered old pedal car with wonky wheels and missing tyres, but to its once-young owner it remains a treasured plaything; a long-remembered doll's pram is brought out, once used to wheel the latest dolly acquisition, or the latest plastic-tyred three-wheeled Dinkie (which still carries the famous name on the fork of the handlebars), that a child or grandchild uses to peform 'wheelies' down the driveway of a modern home.

This seven-lettered word 'Cyclops' has graced both boys' and girls' wheeled toys for over 80 years. There are myriads of Australians who, when little, were wheeled along by fond parents, safely ensconced in the baby carriages proudly emblazoned with the name 'Cyclops'. This trade name has had a profound influence on both the wholesale and retail buying of the Australian public for a great many years.

Having originated in a small way in Sydney and spurred on by the insistence and influence of a child's need, Cyclops progressed from an employment base of 4 people, continuing to grow through the years of World War I, the fabulous 1920s, the bad years of the 1930s Depression, and then under great difficulty and stress during the later years of World War II. Following the revival of industry after the war—when returned servicemen wanted to buy the best for the children that they had left behind—Cyclops came under British ownership. In 1956 the company marketed 100 different items, reaching its zenith in 1968 when the conglomerate it had become marketed over 2000 individual items, (including surfboards, wading pools and slippery slides).

When the first British owner faced bankruptcy in the 1970s, the whole network was taken over by another British conglomerate. In the late 1980s the toys were being manufactured offshore, until the name was rescued by its new owner—an Australian firm—and wheeled toys bearing the name Cyclops are once again manufactured in Australia by Hunter's Toyline. The name 'Cyclops' continues to survive (if only just), against tremendous competition from overseas imports in the 1990s.

This is not just the story of a great Australian icon of childhood—it is a record of the wonderful workmanship and high quality products of the original Australian owner, the merger of an Australian company with a British toy giant, the fall of that great empire, the retrieval, and the endurance of the Cyclops name through it all. For the name of Cyclops lives on, not only in the minds of previous owners, but in the delighted, playful hands of today's children.

'Lal' Smith in his Cyclops 'Star D' pedal car, with 'Whisky' standing on the bonnet (1920s)

Unfortunately, much of the information that would have helped in the recording of these wonderful people who were involved with the establishment of Cyclops in its first 50 years has been lost, and alas, alas, up to now nothing has been available through libraries; therefore it is of the greatest importance that what *is* known today is passed on—before it too, is lost forever.

In my position as Consultant on Toys (particularly those of Australian manufacture) to the Queensland Museum, I have realised the importance of dispersing the knowledge and information that I have amassed over the years through the generosity and tremendous help of some wonderful people throughout Australia, who like myself are interested in preserving our heritage for future generations.

Added to this are my own fond childhood memories of exploring excursions on my beloved red Cyclops No. 3 Scooter, around the streets of West Geelong in Victoria during WWII; later reminiscences—I remember the joy my three sons had with their trusty red Cyclops pedal car in our backyard in Brisbane during the 1960s, and a small granddaughter with her first doll's pram (Cyclops of course) in the early 1980s. All these wonderful memories have made me realise the importance and obvious impact that the word 'Cyclops' has had over the years on just one family.

This book is the result; I hope it will bring back pleasant memories of other childhood years to all readers, young and old.

For the many people who are becoming interested in collecting, restoring and preserving these old toys, I hope you will find the information included in this book to be of great help. Then maybe, just maybe, on reading this, more information will come to light, and even finer examples of these marvellous old childhood icons will be brought forward so that they can be placed in museums where they may be seen for all to enjoy and remember.

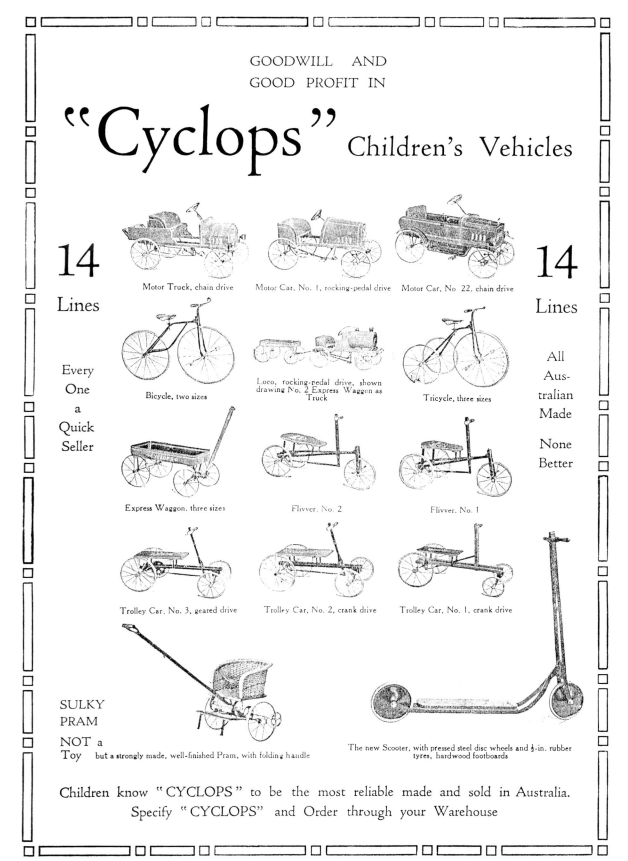

GOODWILL   AND
GOOD   PROFIT   IN

"Cyclops" Children's Vehicles

14
Lines

Every
One
a
Quick
Seller

14
Lines

All
Aus-
tralian
Made

None
Better

Motor Truck, chain drive

Motor Car, No. 1, rocking-pedal drive

Motor Car, No. 22, chain drive

Bicycle, two sizes

Loco, rocking-pedal drive, shown
drawing No. 2 Express Waggon as
Truck

Tricycle, three sizes

Express Waggon, three sizes

Flivver, No. 2

Flivver, No. 1

Trolley Car, No. 3, geared drive

Trolley Car, No. 2, crank drive

Trolley Car, No. 1, crank drive

SULKY
PRAM

NOT a
Toy   but a strongly made, well-finished Pram, with folding handle

The new Scooter, with pressed steel disc wheels and ½-in. rubber
tyres, hardwood footboards

Children know "CYCLOPS" to be the most reliable made and sold in Australia.
Specify "CYCLOPS" and Order through your Warehouse

An original advertisement from The Draper of Australasia Retailers' Handbook and Diary, *1924. (Reproduced
courtesy of Retail House, Brisbane)*

1

1913 Cyclops—The Birth of an Icon

In the early years of this century a large engineering business was situated in Redfern (now an inner city suburb of Sydney), and operated by John Heine. The firm produced sheet metal working machinery, large and small industrial presses, and other appliances of a high standard to assist in the growing industrial strength of factories in an emerging nation, (which until 1901 had been largely dependent on primary production). These machines enabled the production of good cheap uniform products covering a wide variety of articles, whether they were to be stamped or pressed-out of sheet, bar or tube metals.

Such was the high standard of manufacture that many of the metal presses bearing the name John Heine can still be found in use throughout Australia today.

In 1911 the persistent demands of Ernest Heine (the five year old son of John Heine), for an American tricycle led to his father importing one for him. Such was the joy that young Ernest had with this rather odd vehicle, with its solid iron wheels and turned wooden handles, that father John, because of his engineering expertise, saw the future market and had the idea of manufacturing something similar here in Australia. This was the idea which was to grow and evolve again and again over the years, always moving with the times.

In 1913, with a staff of four, John Heine began manufacturing a flat-framed tricycle for children in a small factory at Hay Street, Leichhardt (now an inner suburb of Sydney). By 1915 the name 'Cyclops' had been registered and the new firm had come out with a winning product. It was the Kangaroo Cycle Skate, one of their earliest scooters. It was entirely made out of the best 'cold rolled steel', including the footplate and handles and was finished in black baked enamel. Its bright tinned wheels were 9½" (24 cm) in diameter. With steel wheels it came at 6s 8d (67 cents), but if you wanted such trimmings as

The Kangaroo Cycle Skate of 1915 (Courtesy Australasian Sportsgoods and Toy Retailer)

rubber tyres and a frame finished in bright red enamel, you had to pay 9s (90 cents). Other lines in their 1915 production were simple by today's standards, such as steel hoops.

The year 1917 saw the first mass produced Australian car sold, over 30 years before the production of the Holden. It was a pedal car produced by Cyclops for child motorists. The small car had a rigid and rather angular profile, similar to the angular shape of the full-size cars of the era; this child-sized pedal car was built of seasoned pine timber and sheet metal, with spoked wheels and rubber tyres that were smaller in the front than at the back.

According to a 1921 advertisement from Anthony Horden & Sons Ltd, Universal Providers of Sydney, (who offered a mail order service to their customers all over Australia), the range had grown by then to include the following toys.

A geared handcar or (four-wheeled) trolley—painted, steel frame, cog drive with rubber-tyred wheels that sold for the princely sum of £2 7s 6d ($4.75). An expensive toy for the times.

A similar design with crank drive sold for £1 10s ($3.00) with steel wheels, or £1 6s 6d ($3.65) with rubber tyres.

A similar handcar or trolley (after the style of a railway fettler's trolley), with a wooden frame sold for £1 5s ($2.50) with steel wheels, and £1 11s 6d. ($3.15) with rubber tyres.

A rather elaborate motor locomotive, crank-driven with rubber tyres, sold for £3 15s ($7.50)—more than a week's wages for the average worker at that time.

A chain-driven car with rubber wheels also sold for £3 15s ($7.50), whereas another version of a chain-driven motor car with rubber tyres came complete with lamps and a hooter (horn) in two versions, one at £3 9s 6d ($6.95) and one at £5 ($10.00).

A pullalong four-wheeled waggon (Express Waggon) with an iron body sold in three sizes—13s 6d, 15s 6d, and 18s 3d ($1.35, $1.55, $1.82) with steel wheels; and £1 3s 9d, £1 6s and £1 9s 6d ($2.38, $2.60 and $2.95) with rubber tyres.

The year 1924 marked a milestone in the production of Cyclops pedal cars, when Registered Design No. 4739 was granted to Cyclops on 25 February for the registration of their famous fluted dummy radiator. The registration stated the nature of the design as follows:

Flange-edged stamping in sheet metal displaying a plate with name panel at top and a transversely corrugated panel simulating in appearance the shuttered form of an Automobile Radiator.

In the 1924 edition of the *Draper of Australasia Retailers' Handbook and Diary*, there was an advertisement for Cyclops Children's Vehicles:

—Goodwill and Good Profit—
14 lines
Every one a Quick Seller
—All Australian Made—
None Better
Children know Cyclops to be the most reliable
Made and sold in Australia—Specify 'Cyclops' and
order through your Warehouse.

The power of merchandising was alive and strong even then (see the advertisement on page 10).

Featured in this advertisement was a bicycle, manufactured in two sizes, with a rather unusual frame—somewhere between a bicycle as we have come to know it and an old penny farthing bicycle with the pedals at the bottom of the front forks.

By 1924 Cyclops had also produced a simple catalogue, with the following children's vehicles advertised by way of line drawings:

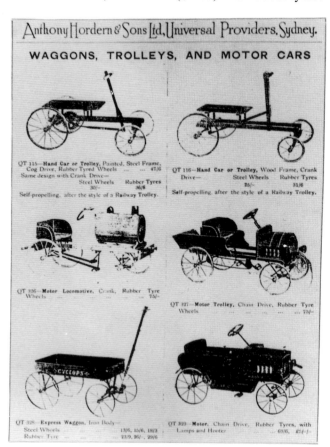

Anthony Hordern & Sons—Sydney advertisment for Cyclops Toys in 1921

Early 1920s vintage Cyclops Motor Truck, complete with Kookaburra hood ornament
(*Courtesy Kath Williams*)

Product	Description
Motor Truck	Chain drive, body painted red or blue, lined, stencilled and varnished; bright tinned wheels,. Will carry two children.
Motor Car No. 0	Crank drive, standard finish red or blue, fitted with headlights, horn and patent disc wheels with rubber tyres. Suitable for children aged three to five.
Motor Car No. 1	Crank drive, standard finish red or blue. Fitted with black enamelled wire wheels.
Motor Car No. 22	Body of seasoned pine and sheet steel, painted red or blue, lined and varnished. Upholstered in red or blue Fabricord. Domed mudguards, nickel-plated mascot.
Motor Car No. 24	Chain drive; standard finish blue, red, grey or brown; upholstered to match. Equipment includes aluminium radiator (registered), bumper, headlights, horn, extra-large steering wheel, windscreen and mascot, wide domed mudguards, aluminium instrument board with embossed clock, speedometer, ammeter and movable switch, plus five extra-strong wire wheels; the Rolls Royce of childhood in the early 1920s.
Locomotive	Crank drive, steers like a motor car. Painted red, blue or green; lined and varnished. Bright tinned wheels and ½" (1¼ cm) rubber tyres.
Tricycles	Frames in baked black enamel; these came in three sizes, with bright tinned wheels. No. 1, No. 2. and No. 3 tricycles all came fitted with either steel or rubber tyres—the first made in Australia and still the best.
Trolley Car No. 1	Crank drive, steel frame with patent reversible front axle; with either steel tyres and wire wheels or rubber tyres and disc wheels.
Trolley Car No. 2	Crank drive, with steel tyres and wire wheels or rubber tyres and wire wheels.
Trolley Car No. 3	Gear drive, with steel tyres and wire wheels or rubber tyres and wire wheels.
The Original Flivver No. 1	Wire wheels and steel tyres or disc wheels and rubber tyres—the most popular toy in Australia.
Flivver No. 2	Wire wheels and steel tyres or with disc wheels and rubber tyres. Large enough for boys up to nine years of age
Scooter	Steel frame, finished in baked black enamel, hardwood footboard, painted red, stencilled and varnished. Disc wheels 7" (18 cm), finished baked red enamel and ½" (1¼ cm) rubber tyres.
Express Waggon No. 1	Measuring 10" x 20" (25½ cm x 51 cm), this was available with either tinned wheels or rubber tyres
Express Waggon No. 2	Measured at 12" x 24" (30½ cm x 61 cm), same finish as No. 1; tinned wheels or rubber tyres
Express Waggon No. 3	Size was 14" x 28" (35½ cm x 71 cm), and came with tinned wheels or rubber tyres;

"CYCLOPS"
Regd.

CHILDREN'S VEHICLES

MOTOR TRUCK

Chain Drive, Bright Tinned Wheels, Body Painted Red or Blue, Lined, Stencilled and Varnished. Will carry 2 children.

PRICE :

CYCLOPS LIMITED
MANUFACTURERS
SYDNEY

"CYCLOPS"
Regd.

LOCOMOTIVE

Price :

Crank Drive, steers like a Motor Car. Painted Red, Blue or Green, Lined and Varnished. Bright tinned Wheels and ½ in Rubber Tyres.

"CYCLOPS"
Regd.

MOTOR CARS

No. 0

Price :

Suitable for children from 3 to 5 years of age.

Crank Drive.

Fitted with patent Disc Wheel's, Rubber Tyres, Headlights and Horn. Standard finish, Red or Blue.

No. 1

Price :

Crank Drive.

Fitted with Black Enamelled Wire Wheels. Standard finish Red or Blue.

"CYCLOPS"
Regd.

MOTOR CAR

No. 24   Price :

Chain Drive. Standard Finish, Blue, Red, Grey or Brown. Upholstered to Match.

EQUIPMENT INCLUDES :- 5 Wire Wheels extra strong, Aluminium Radiator (registered), Bumper, Head Lights, Horn, Extra large Steering Wheel, Windscreen and Mascot, Wide Domed Mudguards, Aluminium Instrument Board with Embossed Clock, Speedometer, Ammeter and Movable Switch.

Pages from a rare and valuable 1924 Cyclops catalogue. The pedal cars depicted include the Motor Truck (top left), models No. 0 and No. 1, (top right), the famous Locomotive (bottom left) and Motor Car No. 24 (bottom right).

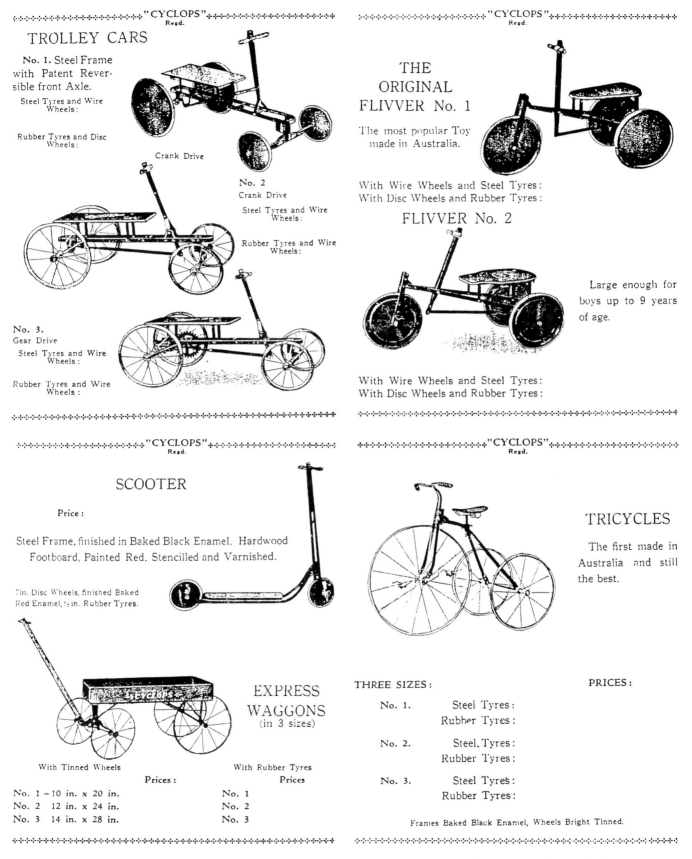

TROLLEY CARS

No. 1. Steel Frame with Patent Reversible front Axle.

Steel Tyres and Wire Wheels:

Rubber Tyres and Disc Wheels:

Crank Drive

No. 2
Crank Drive

Steel Tyres and Wire Wheels:

Rubber Tyres and Wire Wheels:

No. 3.
Gear Drive

Steel Tyres and Wire Wheels:

Rubber Tyres and Wire Wheels:

THE ORIGINAL FLIVVER No. 1

The most popular Toy made in Australia.

With Wire Wheels and Steel Tyres:
With Disc Wheels and Rubber Tyres:

FLIVVER No. 2

Large enough for boys up to 9 years of age.

With Wire Wheels and Steel Tyres:
With Disc Wheels and Rubber Tyres:

SCOOTER

Price:

Steel Frame, finished in Baked Black Enamel. Hardwood Footboard, Painted Red, Stencilled and Varnished.

7in. Disc Wheels, finished Baked Red Enamel, ½in. Rubber Tyres.

EXPRESS WAGGONS
(in 3 sizes)

With Tinned Wheels
Prices:

		With Rubber Tyres Prices
No. 1 – 10 in. x 20 in.		No. 1
No. 2 12 in. x 24 in.		No. 2
No. 3 14 in. x 28 in.		No. 3

TRICYCLES

The first made in Australia and still the best.

		PRICES:
THREE SIZES:		
No. 1.	Steel Tyres:	
	Rubber Tyres:	
No. 2.	Steel Tyres:	
	Rubber Tyres:	
No. 3.	Steel Tyres:	
	Rubber Tyres:	

Frames Baked Black Enamel, Wheels Bright Tinned.

Also from the 1924 catalogue—a selection of trolley cars (top left), Flivvers (top right), scooters (bottom left) and a vintage tricycle available in three sizes (bottom left).

Also featured was a sulky pram (or stroller) made of cane, with a folding handle; it was not a toy, but a strong serviceable pram. A toy version was available in the 1930s.

By 1926 Cyclops merchandise had spread Australia-wide, with their goods being included in advertising by the large Brisbane department store McWhirters, of Fortitude Valley, and also in the Bairds general catalogue No. 7 in Western Australia.

The lines these two stores expected to be the best sellers, were the Cyclops 'Express Waggons', with their four steel wheels and iron body and the trolley cars (or Pull Waggons as they were called by McWhirters), with their lever drive. These were steered with the rider's feet on the front axle, and they were available with either fitted rubber-tyred disc wheels or spoked wheels with steel tyres. Both versions were constructed on a very strong frame and nicely finished. Size No. 1 had 11" (28 cm) rear wheels and sold for the princely sum of £1 15s ($3.50) in Western Australia and £1 5s ($2.50) in Queensland. No. 2 had 14" (35½ cm) rear wheels and sold for £1 19s 6d ($3.95) and £1 10s ($3.00) in Western Australia and Queensland respectively. The rubber-tyred versions were No. 1 at £2 6s ($4.25) in WA and £1 15s ($3.50) in Queensland, and No. 2 at £2 7s 6d ($4.75) in WA and £2 ($4.00) in Queensland. These variations give an insight into the effect that distance had on prices.

Also featured were the Flivvers, with their all steel frames; a popular and useful toy worked by hand-lever, with steel-tyred wheel and rubber-tyred disc wheel versions also available. The ever-popular tricycle was, of course available in its three sizes; No. 1 had a 16" (40½ cm) front wheel; No. 2, a 20" (51 cm) front wheel and No. 3 had a 22" (56 cm) front wheel—all three came in rubber-tyred or steel rim versions.

Because of the high demand for its products throughout Australia, the Cyclops factory moved to 24 William Street, Leichhardt in 1926 (with the Postal address of PO Box 17).

The head office of Cyclops remained there for about sixty years; the actual building with the Cyclops name clearly emblazoned on it was still standing in March 1995 until the head office was moved to Melbourne in Victoria under Britax (a division of Tube Industries), in the late 1980s. In the early 1990s Hunter's Toyline bought the name 'Cyclops', and a small wheeled toy line bearing the famous name is now manufactured in the Hunter's Toyline factory in Victoria.

An application for Patent No. 6046/27 was lodged for improvements to axle mountings for Flivvers and other light wheeled structures on 21 February 1927, and granted on 26 July.

Jack Gray, seated on his Flivver, which he called his 'whizzer' in the mid-1920s. (Courtesy of Mrs A. B. Moores and Jack Gray)

The first mention that I have been able to find so far of the famous Cyclops Dinkie (or small three-wheeled trike for young children), is the notation of the 'Cyclops Dinkie Car' in the 1928 advertisement of The Bairds Co. Ltd, of Western Australia; it stated that this three-wheeled vehicle was strong and easy to drive. (It is interesting to note that a somewhat similar Dinkie was still being manufactured and sold in 1950, so popular was this design).

Although Cyclops was by this time receiving a great deal of competition from both overseas companies (such as Hutchem, Robsonia and Tri-ang), and Australian companies such as Eclipse, Heine's company was still able to hold their own in the wheeled toy market.

A new form of pedal car was registered by Cyclops on 5 June 1929, being Registration No. 7662; it was a Toy Aero-Tricycle. The nature of design specified:

'A fuselage-like body with mock radiator front, with a propeller fitted in front of it; above the cowl a mock wing, at the tail a mock vertical rudder; three-wheel undergear comprising a pair of Ackerman jointed front wheels, single rear wheel with pedal drive to a crank pin thereon. The design is applicable for the pattern, shape configuration of a Toy Aero-Tricycle by stamping, bending and of sheet and bar metal.'

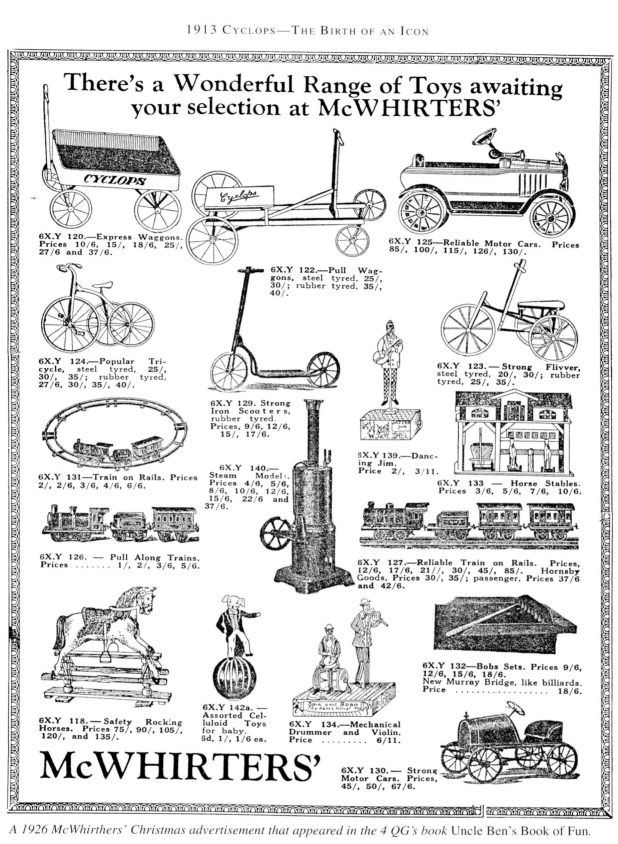

A 1926 McWhirthers' Christmas advertisement that appeared in the 4 QG's book Uncle Ben's Book of Fun.

2

1930s More Than Just a Toy

With the onset of the thirties the firm of Cyclops designed and developed more and more vehicles to add to their ever-growing line of wheeled toys, including pedal cars, tricycles, 'Dinkies', scooters and waggons. Although the latter were primarily designed with boys in

Built to last—Lorie Ulrick in his 1931/32 Cyclops Model No. 1 pedal car

mind they were enjoyed by girls as well. Soon however, the sisters of the boys were accommodated with their own Cyclops wheeled toys; namely, a small range of doll's prams and pushers (or sulkies). Child-sized wheelbarrows were also manufactured so that young children could work and play alongside their parents in the garden.

The Cyclops design department tried at all times to keep abreast of the many new full-size motor cars which were then appearing on the streets of Australia; they realised that children insist on realism, so wherever it was possible Cyclops tried to mimic the lines of the new adult cars (simplified, of course), when making the latest in pedal cars. The designers were very much aware of children's interest in the different makes of cars, and therefore built the pedal cars with bumper bars, bulging balloon tyres and the latest in streamlining.

Nearly every year a new type of pedal car would be introduced into the Cyclops range, following the latest whims of the adult cars. Six or more cars would often be designed, but only two or so would ever be passed for mass production. When test cars were made from these new designs, they were not only examined by a highly critical board of directors but also by their greatest critics— a group of youngsters themselves. The board would gain important information on consumer reaction by inviting children to the factory to play with the new pedal cars, and asking them to decide which they liked the best. All of this was done before a new model went into production.

Many of the pedal cars of this era were built with almost the same heavy gauge of steel as the adult-sized cars, and this is the reason why so many of the 1930s to 1950s

Cyclops pedal cars survive today. They may be a little rusted and dented and a trifle worse for wear, but with love and a lot of energy, they can be returned to their marvellous original condition, just like their full-size veteran and vintage counterparts.

A 1930s advertisement that I came across from F. Tritton, Home Furnishers, once situated at 260 George Street in Brisbane (now long gone), advertised:

Motor cars, real beauties, just what boys and girls want. Buicks, Hudsons, Federal, Dodge, Packard, Willy-Knight and Chrysler, and Fire Brigade Motors with real dinky ladders and a big bell—just like the regular fireman's car. Each car is guaranteed to do no less than sixty miles to the gallon. Speed?? Well, there is no limit. You can go your hardest—if you get ahead of dad's car, he won't like it—so I'd advise—keep well behind him. The price is nothing like that of dad's car—that's hopeful, isn't it?

Prices ranged from £4 10s ($9.00) to £14 15s ($29.50)—a heavenly sum indeed in those days, when many men's wages were around £5 ($10.00) a week, if they were lucky. Tricycles for boys and girls from 5 to 9 years of age were built of steel tube with ball bearings, rubber tyres, rustless spokes, nickel fittings and solid tyres; they ranged in price from £2 12s 6d ($5.25) to £5 17s 6d ($11.75). Speed bicycles for boys and girls cost £5 7s 6d ($10.75), and scooters with ball bearings were priced at both £2 5s and £2 10s ($4.50 and $5.00).

While the 1920s pedal cars that were featured in advertisements and catalogues had been sold by numbers such as Nos 0, 1, 22 or 24, the 1930s models were given up-to-date names such as the Cyclops 'Straight 8 Car', or even the names of famous full-size motor cars, such as 'Chevrolet' and 'Chrysler'.

In a 1930 catalogue from Bairds Co. Ltd (of Western Australia), the following Cyclops toys were listed:

'Star' Motor Car—Length 30" (76 cm) for children aged three to five years. Red enamelled and strongly constructed, fitted with rubber tyres; priced at £2 2s 6d ($4.25).

Wheelbarrows with a steel tray, a rubber-tyred blue disc wheel and a red body measured 27" (68½ cm) in length and sold for 9s 6d (95 cents).

'Straight 8 Car'—With a length of 44" (112 cm) and 11" (28 cm) balloon disc wheels, cycle-chain drive, a lacquer finish, plated radiator and efficient brakes, this model came complete with horn, headlights and windscreen; it sold for £7 5s ($14.50)

Anthony Hordens' Christmas Gift and Toy Book of 1931 advertised a sturdy Dinkie with 9" (23 cm) balloon disc wheels for £1 ($2.00). Also advertised was the Cyclops bicycle for the boy who has outgrown his tricycle; fitted with ½" (1¼ cm) rubber tyres, the 20" (51 cm) wheel size model sold for £1 10s ($3.00) and the 22" (56 cm) wheel size was priced at £1 14s ($3.40).

The 'Cyclobike' made its first appearance during this era, with a tubular frame, ball bearings throughout, free wheel, front wheel brakes and heavy rubber tyres; it sold for £3 19s 6d ($7.95). The tricycles, scooters and Express Waggons were still firm favourites.

An impressive lineup; John McCarthy in the 'Packard' on the left (Barbara Lahey as passenger), Alicia Lahey in a 1930s Cyclops 'Pontiac' pedal car and Geoffrey Lahey in a late 1930s Peerless truck.

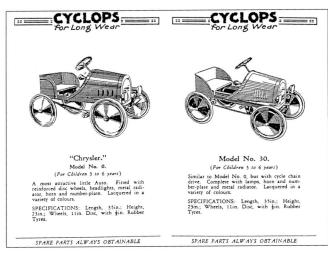

"Chrysler."
Model No. 0.
(For Children 3 to 6 years)

A most attractive little Auto. Fitted with reinforced disc wheels, headlights, metal radiator, horn and number-plate. Lacquered in a variety of colours.

SPECIFICATIONS: Length, 35in.; Height, 23in.; Wheels, 11in. Disc, with 1/2 in. Rubber Tyres.

SPARE PARTS ALWAYS OBTAINABLE

Model No. 30.
(For Children 3 to 6 years)

Similar to Model No. 0, but with cycle chain drive. Complete with lamps, horn and number-plate and metal radiator. Lacquered in a variety of colours.

SPECIFICATIONS: Length, 35in.; Height, 23in.; Wheels, 11in. Disc, with 1/2 in. Rubber Tyres.

SPARE PARTS ALWAYS OBTAINABLE

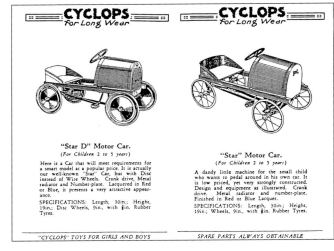

"Star D" Motor Car.
(For Children 2 to 5 years)

Here is a Car that will meet requirements for a smart model at a popular price. It is actually our well-known "Star" Car, but with Disc instead of Wire Wheels. Crank drive, Metal radiator and Number-plate. Lacquered in Red or Blue, it presents a very attractive appearance.

SPECIFICATIONS: Length, 30in.; Height, 19in.; Disc Wheels, 9in., with 1/2 in. Rubber Tyres.

"CYCLOPS" TOYS FOR GIRLS AND BOYS

"Star" Motor Car.
(For Children 2 to 5 years)

A dandy little machine for the small child who wants to pedal around in his own car. It is low priced, yet very strongly constructed. Design and equipment as illustrated. Crank drive. Metal radiator and number-plate. Finished in Red or Blue Lacquer.

SPECIFICATIONS: Length, 30in.; Height, 19in.; Wheels, 9in., with 1/2 in. Rubber Tyres.

SPARE PARTS ALWAYS OBTAINABLE

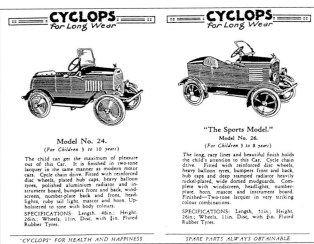

Model No. 24.
(For Children 3 to 10 years)

The child can get the maximum of pleasure out of this Car. It is finished in two-tone lacquer in the same manner as modern motor cars. Cycle chain drive. Fitted with reinforced disc wheels, plated hub caps, heavy balloon tyres, polished aluminium radiator and instrument board, bumpers front and back, windscreen, number-plate back and front, headlights, ruby tail light, mascot and horn. Upholstered to tone with body colours.

SPECIFICATIONS: Length, 48in.; Height, 26in.; Wheels, 11in. Disc, with 1/2 in. Fluted Rubber Tyres.

"CYCLOPS" FOR HEALTH AND HAPPINESS

"The Sports Model."
Model No. 26.
(For Children 3 to 8 years)

The long, racy lines and beautiful finish holds the child's attention to this Car. Cycle chain drive. Fitted with reinforced disc wheels, heavy balloon tyres, bumpers front and back, hub caps and deep stamped radiator heavily nickel-plated, wide domed mudguards. Complete with windscreen, headlights, number-plate, horn, mascot and instrument board. Finished—Two-tone lacquer in very striking colour combinations.

SPECIFICATIONS: Length, 51in.; Height, 26in.; Wheels, 11in. Disc, with 1/2 in. Fluted Rubber Tyres.

SPARE PARTS ALWAYS OBTAINABLE

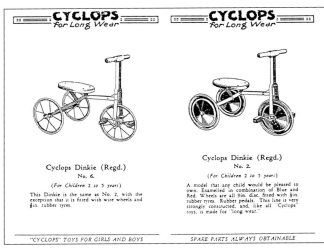

Cyclops Dinkie (Regd.)
No. 6.
(For Children 2 to 5 years)

This Dinkie is the same as No. 2, with the exception that it is fitted with wire wheels and 1/2 in. rubber tyres.

"CYCLOPS" TOYS FOR GIRLS AND BOYS

Cyclops Dinkie (Regd.)
No. 2.
(For Children 2 to 5 years)

A model that any child would be pleased to own. Enamelled in combination of Blue and Red. Wheels are all 9in. disc, fitted with 1/2 in. rubber tyres. Rubber pedals. This line is very strongly constructed, and, like all "Cyclops" toys, is made for "long wear."

SPARE PARTS ALWAYS OBTAINABLE

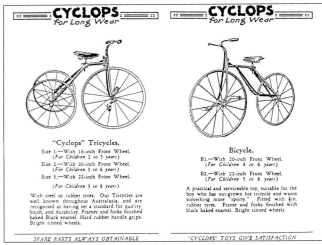

"Cyclops" Tricycles.

Size 1.—With 16-inch Front Wheel.
(For Children 2 to 5 years)
Size 2.—With 20-inch Front Wheel.
(For Children 3 to 6 years)
Size 3.—With 22-inch Front Wheel.
(For Children 3 to 8 years)

With steel or rubber tyres. Our Tricycles are well known throughout Australasia, and are recognised as having set a standard for quality finish, and durability. Frames and forks finished baked Black enamel. Hard rubber handle grips. Bright tinned wheels.

SPARE PARTS ALWAYS OBTAINABLE

Bicycle.

B1.—With 20-inch Front Wheel.
(For Children 4 to 6 years)
B2.—With 22-inch Front Wheel.
(For Children 5 to 8 years)

A practical and serviceable toy, suitable for the boy who has out-grown his tricycle and wants something more "sporty." Fitted with 1/2 in. rubber tyres. Frame and forks finished with black baked enamel. Bright tinned wheels.

"CYCLOPS" TOYS GIVE SATISFACTION

Pages from the 1932 Cyclops catalogue, including the cover.

Although they may have been commercially available beforehand (no definite data is available on this as yet), 1932 appears to be the year that the marvellous Cyclops 'Aeroplane' and the 'Cyclops Motor Truck' were first advertised. They appeared along with a growing range of vehicles in the company's own 1932 trade catalogue, which was released with the slogan 'Cyclops for Long

CYCLOPS
— MADE IN AUSTRALIA —

1932

A Cyclops waggon on the left and a 1930s pedal car (Courtesy of Heather M. Hiley)

Wear'. Included in this catalogue were the following pedal cars:

'Chevrolet' (Model OOD)
'Chevrolet' (Model No. 00)
'Star D' Motor Car
'Star' Motor Car
'Chrysler' (Model No. 0)
Model No. 30
Model No. 1
Model No. 28
'Straight Eight' (Model No. 31)
Model No. 24
'Sports Model' (Model No. 26)
'Aeroplane'
'Cyclops Motor Truck'.

Many of the cars were completely updated versions of their 1924 counterparts.

The range of Cyclops Dinkies (by this time, 'Dinkie' was a registered trademark), was also increasing and included Dinkie No. 2, Nos 4, 5, and 6, and also the 'Dinkie Express'. Only one of these—Dinkie No. 6—was fitted with wire wheels and $^3/_8$" (1 cm) rubber tyres; the rest were fitted with disc wheels and rubber tyres and they also had rubber pedals.

The famous Cyclops tricycle was still available in sizes 1, 2 and 3, but 6 and 7 had been added to the range, along with what could possibly be the first tubular tricycles— Nos 4 and 5.

For the older boys, the Cyclops bicycle came in two sizes—B1 and B2. There was also the 'Boy's Bicycle No. 3' and the 'Scootabike' (Registered design).

Flivvers No. 1 and No. 2 continued to be manufactured along with the No. 4 'Express Waggon' and the wheelbarrow.

There were now eight different scooters in the range— No. 1, No. 2, the 'DeLuxe' No. 3, No. 4, No. 5, No. 6 (which had two back wheels, making it safe for the small child), and No. 7—all with disc wheels; Scooter No. 8, had nickel-plated hubs, tangent spokes and cushion tyres.

Although girls often played with their brother's Cyclops toys, they were now especially catered for with two dolls' prams—No. 1 and No. 2—the bodies were made of steel, with collapsible and strong material hoods. There was also a doll's cot made of steel.

Along with these articles was a folding garden chair; it was intended for children and was also a handy line for motorists and campers. It was made with a steel frame and had a wooden seat and back.

Cyclops Limited made an application for a Patent— No. 17,508/34, for 'improvements in scooter toys', invented by Philip Guyton Tucker of New South Wales, (who also invented the improved axle mountings for Flivvers in 1927). The invention put forward to patent was in fact 'to reduce wear and tear and ensure smoother running of the vehicle (scooter), and to that end it consists in spring mounting the platform on the frame in a practical arrangement in which the platform is tiltable vertically about a pivot bearing at the rear end of it, and at its fore end is born on springs which absorb road shocks and permit it an appropriate freedom for vertical oscillation'— in short, the invention gave the scooter a sprung footboard.

A Cyclops advertisement (appearing some time between the years 1934 and 1936), showed a line of cars which included the 'Rover', the 'Standard' and the 'Hillman', but there is a query as to when and if they were actually mass produced, or whether their radiators were altered and reproduced under another name. The rest of the cars in the advertisement, namely the models No. 0, No. 30, No. 31 and the 'Cyclops Motor Truck', were all included in the company's 1932 catalogue. The Cyclops 'Aeroplane' appears to have been improved and renamed 'The Cyclops Centenary Flyer' in honour of the Centenary Air Race from England to Australia, and a new truck had also been added—the 'Bedford' motor truck.

A Cyclops toys Christmas advertisement in 1936 shows the evolving shape of the pedal cars, with a brand new radiator shape on most of the cars. The tremendous influence of the American automobile on Australian society can also be gauged, with pedal cars bearing the names 'Plymouth', 'Pontiac', 'Dodge', 'Oldsmobile', 'Chrysler', 'Buick' and 'Packard'. Only one of the two trucks bore an English brand name—the 'Bedford'. Many of these American-style names were still found in the early 1940s catalogues, but by the early 1950s they had disappeared.

A Cyclops 'DeLuxe' model car was advertised in 1937, with chain-drive, mudguards, running board, headlamps, horn, windscreen, bumper bars, number plate, tail light and an adjustable seat. It was 49" x 22" (124½ x 56 cm) in size, with 9" (23 cm) rubber-tyred wheels. The car was available in red or blue and suitable for children aged four to eight years.

The Myer Emporium in Melbourne advertised a strongly constructed doll's pram for £1 4s 6d ($2.45) in November 1937. Constructed of wood with a collapsible hood, a heavy steel under-carriage and 7" (18 cm) rubber-tyred wheels, it was lacquered in navy or maroon. I had one of these prams in my possession until a few years ago; it was lacquered maroon, but without the material on the hood. Bought in Ballarat, the pram proudly displayed the famous Cyclops trademark between the handlebars. I have searched for many years for further information on the span of years that this small wooden-bodied pram was manufactured by Cyclops, because although another larger wooden pram was featured in the 1940 and 1941 catalogues, all my other information points to the manufacture of metal prams during this time.

What a range of Cyclops toys there were in the 1938 catalogue—if only you had the money. The 'Plymouth',

A series of pre-Christmas advertisements by Myer's of Melbourne in 1937

'Pontiac', 'Dodge', 'Oldsmobile', 'Chrysler' and 'Buick' pedal cars were featured; the 'Bedford' and 'Cyclops Motor Truck' were still being manufactured, but a newcomer was now on the scene—the wonderful 'Packard', complete with a folding 'dickey seat' for that extra passenger. It was chain-driven with streamlined mudguards, horn, handbrake, windscreen, mascot, instrument board, headlights, tail light, number plate and nickel-plated bumper bars.

Tricycles 1, 2 and 3 were still being manufactured along with Nos 8, 9, 10, 11 and 12, all in various shapes and configurations: the tubular tricycles Nos 4 and 5 were also still on the scene.

The 'Juvenile Bicycle No. 3' and No. 4 had taken over from their three predecessors, and were suitable for children from five to ten years of age.

The ever-popular Dinkie was produced in five variations; No. 1 and No. 6 with spoked wheels, and Nos 4, 5 and 7 with disc wheels were the first two designs. The 'Trailer Trike' had spoked wheels. These were joined by the wonderful 'Pedal Pony', with a body realistically carved from a solid piece of wood. It came complete with

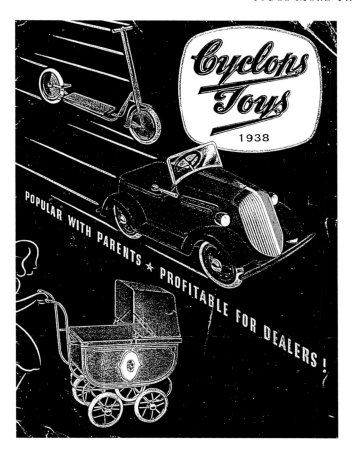

"THE CHRYSLER"

(For children 4 to 8 years)

Adjustable Seat

Ball Bearings

MEASUREMENTS—Length, 46 inches. Height, 22 inches.

SPECIFICATIONS—Body and chassis constructed entirely of steel. Rigid and strong. Stamped streamlined mudguards. Adjustable seat. Chain enclosed in heavy metal cover. Back axle runs on ball bearings.

FINISH—Body stove enamelled in red or blue. Striped in white. Mudguards enamelled to match.

EQUIPMENT—Cycle chain drive. Cast steering wheel. Modern streamlined radiator. Horn. Head lights. Mascot. Number plate. Tail light. Nickel plated bumper bars. Windscreen. Instrument board.

WHEELS—9 inch stamped steel spoke with ⅞ inch rubber tyres, enamelled to match body. Large nickel plated hub caps.

Weight, 46 lbs.

SPARE PARTS ALWAYS OBTAINABLE

4

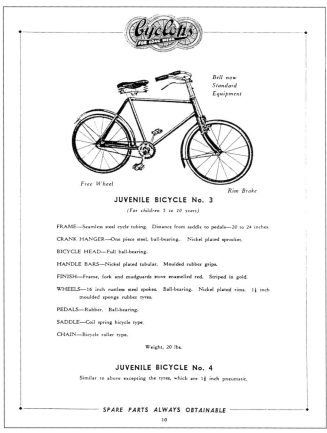

Bell now Standard Equipment

Free Wheel

Rim Brake

JUVENILE BICYCLE No. 3

(For children 5 to 10 years)

FRAME—Seamless steel cycle tubing. Distance from saddle to pedals—20 to 24 inches.

CRANK HANGER—One piece steel, ball-bearing. Nickel plated sprocket.

BICYCLE HEAD—Full ball-bearing.

HANDLE BARS—Nickel plated tubular. Moulded rubber grips.

FINISH—Frame, fork and mudguards stove enamelled red. Striped in gold.

WHEELS—16 inch rustless steel spokes. Ball-bearing. Nickel plated rims. 1¼ inch moulded sponge rubber tyres.

PEDALS—Rubber. Ball-bearing.

SADDLE—Coil spring bicycle type.

CHAIN—Bicycle roller type.

Weight, 20 lbs.

JUVENILE BICYCLE No. 4

Similar to above excepting the tyres, which are 1¼ inch pneumatic.

SPARE PARTS ALWAYS OBTAINABLE

10

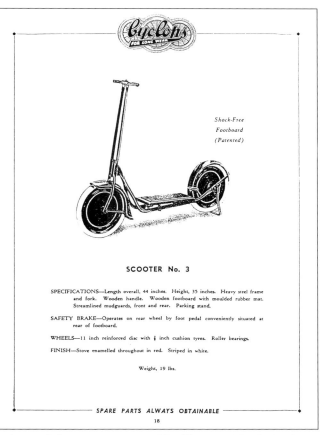

Shock-Free Footboard (Patented)

SCOOTER No. 3

SPECIFICATIONS—Length overall, 44 inches. Height, 35 inches. Heavy steel frame and fork. Wooden handle. Wooden footboard with moulded rubber mat. Streamlined mudguards, front and rear. Parking stand.

SAFETY BRAKE—Operates on rear wheel by foot pedal conveniently situated at rear of footboard.

WHEELS—11 inch reinforced disc with ⅞ inch cushion tyres. Roller bearings.

FINISH—Stove enamelled throughout in red. Striped in white.

Weight, 19 lbs.

SPARE PARTS ALWAYS OBTAINABLE

18

Pages from the 1938 Cyclops catalogue; the cover depicted a racing pedal car, a scooter and Doll's Pram No. 2. By this time, the wheeled toy range had expanded to include two-wheeled bicycles.

reins and a saddle, on a steel frame with steel front fork. The body of the pony was finished in dapple grey, with the undergear and wheels enamelled red.

There were nine scooters in the range, including No. 3 (which the shock-free patented footboard), Nos 4 and 5, and No. 6, which had two back wheels to stabilise it—it was designed for younger children. Nos 7, 10 and 11 were also around, as was No. 12 (the 'Scooter DeLuxe', with wire-spoked wheels, a bell and pneumatic tyres), and No. 14 which also had pneumatic tyres, but with disc wheels.

Doll's Pram No. 1 was available in the following colour combinations: sky blue, fawn or pink. Each variation was produced with a cream panelled decoration. Doll's Pram No. 2 had the same colour schemes as No. 1 although it was 2" (5 cm) longer, wider and deeper The doll's cot was available lacquered in either blue or pink, with a neat transfer at the foot of each cot. A 'Strollette' (doll's stroller) was made of the best quality pine, fitted with arm rests and body strap, and available finished in blue, green or orange, with striped deck chair canvas to tone. It was obtainable with or without the folding hood (which cost extra).

There were two sizes of wheelbarrows available and also two Waggons—No. 4 and No. 5.

A Cyclops Toys Christmas advertisement, circa 1936.

Barbara Hancock with her beloved Pedal Pony; she used to 'feed' her pony vegetable peelings on a tin plate. The wheels, saddle and handlebars were red, the body dappled grey and cream, and the reins were brown. By the 1940s, this toy cost £1 16s 6d ($3.65).

In the Bairds Coy. Ltd (Perth, WA) catalogue No. 10, dated August 1939 (only a month before the outbreak of WW II), Bairds featured a large range of Cyclops toys and also Cyclops 'Child's Stroller No. 1' (which had a wooden frame) and No. 2 (steel-framed with a protecting hood flap). The Cyclops all-steel stroller with completely enclosed canvas sides also featured, as did the No. 4 Child's Stroller—all for the actual child. No. 2 and No. 4 had adjustable drop backs, and all were finished with colourful striped cotton canvas. A doll's strollette, a smaller version of the No. 1 child's stroller, was also available and this same stroller was also featured in a Harris Scarfe & Sandovers Ltd advertisement from about the same period.

Before proceeding to the next chapter which covers the trials and tribulations faced by Cyclops during the next decade, some tables of products, defined by copies of catalogues and advertisements in my possession follows. The tables include those products that were manufactured by Cyclops from the 1930s up until 1941. Also included are the actual numbers of each article manufactured during the first eight months of 1941, before the strict regulations demanded by the War Organisation of Industry (W.O.I.), came into force.

PRODUCT	1932	1936–38	1940	1941	Total Manufactured in 1941
PEDAL CARS					
Chrysler	1932				
Model No. 30	1932	1936/38			
Model No. 1	1932				
Chevrolet Model 00D	1932				
Chevrolet Model No. 00	1932				
Star D Motor Car	1932				
Star Motor Car	1932				
Model No. 28	1932				
Straight 8 (No. 31)	1932	1936/38			
Model No. 24	1932				
Sports Model No. 26	1932				
The Aeroplane	1932				
Centenary Flyer		1936/38			
Cyclops Motor Truck	1932	1936/38			
Rover Motor Car		1936/38?			
Standard Motor Car		1936/38?			
Hillman Motor Car		1936/38?			
Model No. 0		1936/38			
The Plymouth		1938			
The Pontiac		1938	1940	1941	3857
The Dodge		1938			
The Oldsmobile		1938	1940	1941	1068
The Chrysler		1938	1940	1941	776
The Buick		1938	1940		
The Packard		1938	1940	1941	459
The Bedford		1936/38			
Cyclops Motor Truck		1936/38	1940	1941	404
The Chevrolet			1940	1941	4256
Sports V-8			1940	1941	2540
The Vauxhall			1940	1941	1088
The Reo (Truck)			1940	1941	2463
Armoured Car			1940	1941	330
DINKIES					
Dinkie No. 5	1932	1936/38	1940	1941	9439
Dinkie No. 4	1932	1936/38	1940	1941	12, 687
Dinkie No. 6	1932	1936/38			
Dinkie No. 2	1932	1936/38			
Dinkie Express	1932		1940	1941	7400
Dinkie No. 00		1936/38			
Dinkie No. 1		1936/38			
Dinkie No. 3		1936/38			
TRICYCLES					
Trailer Trike		1936/38	1940	1941	4171
Tricycle No. 6	1932	1936/38			
Tricycle No. 7	1932	1936/38			
Tricycle Size 1	1932	1936/38	1940	1941	3155
Size 2	1932	1936/38	1940	1941	2412
Size 3	1932	1936/38	1940	1941	1237
Tubular Tricycle No. 4	1932	1936/38	1940	1941	282
No. 5	1932	1936/38	1940	1941	241
Tricycle No. 8		1936/38	1940		196
Tricycle No. 9		1936/38	1940		185
Tricycle No. 10		1938	1940		103

PRODUCT	1932	1936–38	1940	1941	Total Manufactured in 1941
Tricycle No. 11		1938	1940	1941	3977
Tricycle No. 12		1938	1940	1941	3687
Tricycle No. 14				1941	1154
Tricycle No. 15				1941	1427
Tricycle No. 16				1941	917
Tricycle No. 18				1941	1146
Tricycle No. 19				1941	1396
Tricycle No. 20				1941	870
BIKES AND FLIVVERS					
Cyclops Sidecar			1940	1941	751
Cyclobike				1941	990
Bicycle B.1	1924 1932	1936/38			
B.2	1932	1936/38			
Flivver No. 1	1932	1936/38	1940	1941	180
No. 2	1932	1936/38	1940	1941	123
SCOOTERS					
Scooter No. 1	1932				
Scooter DeLuxe No. 3	1932	1936/38	1940		5108
Scooter No. 4	1932	1936/38	1940	1941	3366
Scooter No. 5	1932	1936/38	1940	1941	2459
Scooter No. 6	1932	1936/38	1940	1941	2633
Scooter No. 7	1932	1936/38	1940	1941	2271
Scooter No. 8	1932	1936/38			
Scooter No. 9		1936/38			
Scooter No. 10		1936/38	1940		3955
Scooter No. 11		1936/38	1940		873
Scooter No. 12		1938	1940	1941	316
Scooter No. 14		1938	1940	1941	1006
Scooter No. 15				1941	1884
DOLL PRODUCTS					
Pram No. 1	1932	1936/38	1940	1941	5578
Pram No. 2	1932	1936/38	1940	1941	3354
Pram No. 3			1940	1941	355
Cot	1932	1936/38			17
Strollette		1938	1940	1941	8290
Tools, Waggons & others					
Wheelbarrow No. 1		1938	1940	1941	5013
No. 2		1938	1940	1941	3299
Waggon No. 4		1938	1940	1941	3413
Waggon No. 5		1938	1940	1941	2753
Waggon No. 0			1940	1941	9848
Lawnmower No. 1			1940	1941	11137
Lawnmower No. 2			1940	1941	4030
Garden Tools			1940	1941	12143
Beach Spade				1941	10105
Tin Helmet			1940	1941	37164
Bizzie-Bee Carpet Sweeper				1941	
Pedal Pony		1936/38	1940	1941	2465

By August 1941, Cyclops had completely sold out their supplies on hand, and shortages due to the war meant that production was curtailed.

Graeme Love in his brand new Centenary Flyer, (1935)—a very young 'Biggles'

Christmas in 1937—this lucky young chap received a red Cyclops 'Chrysler' with silver trim.

3

1940s The War Years—W.O.I Problems

The beginning of the 1940s found the firm of Cyclops, like many other Australian firms, rather short of manpower. This was due to so many of their employees enlisting for service in the armed forces—but Cyclops were still manufacturing as much as possible to fill the gap in a market that was grievously under-supplied. This was mainly due to the fact that Australian firms had to supply the overseas demand for goods, as the war in Europe meant that the disunited continent was running short of just about everything.

According to my data, the output for 1941 was not as great as that of the whole year of 1938. However, considering that the figures for 1941 (refer to the tables in the previous chapter), only represent the production up to August of that year, the overall figures (62, 681 wheeled toys and 90, 060 items in the 'small toy' category), are quite significant even by today's standards of mass production. This is particularly impressive in light of the fact that Australia's population in the early 1940s was between seven and eight million people.

It is interesting that even with the outbreak of war, Cyclops still introduced new models to their already extensive range of pre-war toys; the 'Chevrolet', 'Sports V-8', 'Vauxhall', 'Reo Truck' and 'Armoured Car' all featured in their 1940 catalogue, but not in their 1938 version. One extra Dinkie was also added to the range, plus four extra tricycles, including the Cyclops 'Sidecar'. An additional seven trikes were added in 1941, but the variety of scooters decreased; a wooden doll's pram was in evidence in the 1940 catalogue.

In the small toy category there was quite a difference,

The Cyclops Toys wholesale price list from March to June of 1940 provides a full list of their lines at that time.

with the small 'Waggon No. 0', two new toy lawnmowers, garden toys and the popular toy 'Tin Helmet' all found in the 1940 catalogue. A beach spade and a toy carpet sweeper were added to the 1941 catalogue.

CHILDREN'S
VEHICLES *and*
SMALL TOYS

1941

Manufactured by
CYCLOPS TOYS PTY. LTD.
Factory & Showrooms:
WILLIAM STREET, LEICHHARDT
N.S.W.
'Phones: LM 1414 (3 lines)
Registered Telegraphic Address:
"CYCLOPSTOYS SYDNEY"

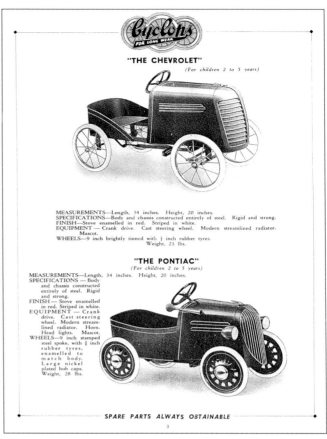

"THE CHEVROLET"
(For children 2 to 5 years)

MEASUREMENTS—Length, 34 inches. Height, 20 inches.
SPECIFICATIONS—Body and chassis constructed entirely of steel. Rigid and strong.
FINISH—Stove enamelled in red. Striped in white.
EQUIPMENT—Crank drive. Cast steering wheel. Modern streamlined radiator. Mascot.
WHEELS—9 inch brightly tinned with ⅜ inch rubber tyres.
Weight, 23 lbs.

"THE PONTIAC"
(For children 2 to 5 years)

MEASUREMENTS—Length, 34 inches. Height, 20 inches.
SPECIFICATIONS — Body and chassis constructed entirely of steel. Rigid and strong.
FINISH — Stove enamelled in red. Striped in white.
EQUIPMENT — Crank drive. Cast steering wheel. Modern streamlined radiator. Horn. Head lights. Mascot.
WHEELS—9 inch stamped steel spoke, with ⅜ inch rubber tyres, enamelled to match body. Large nickel plated hub caps.
Weight, 28 lbs.

SPARE PARTS ALWAYS OBTAINABLE
3

"THE PACKARD"
(For children 4 to 8 years)

Folding Dickey Seat

Brake

Ball Bearings

MEASUREMENTS—Length, 52 inches. Height, 24 inches.

SPECIFICATIONS—Body and chassis constructed entirely of steel. Rigid and strong. Stamped streamlined mudguards. Chain enclosed in metal cover. Roomy folding dickey seat. Back axle runs on ball bearings.

FINISH—Body stove enamelled in cream. Striped in red. Mudguards enamelled red.

ELECTRIC HEAD LIGHTS—Fitted with 3.5 volt lamps wired to push and pull switch on dash and to fitting on chassis made to take an Eveready Battery size No. 800. Battery itself not supplied.

EQUIPMENT—Hand brake. Modern streamlined radiator. Cycle chain drive. Horn. Cast steering wheel. Mascot. Number plate. Tail light. Nickel plated bumper bars. Windscreen. Instrument board. Moulded rubber step mats.

WHEELS—10 inch stamped steel spoke, with ⅜ inch rubber tyres, enamelled cream. Large nickel plated hub caps.

Weight, 71 lbs.

SPARE PARTS ALWAYS OBTAINABLE
7

"ARMOURED CAR"
(For children 3 to 7 years)

Ball Bearings

MEASUREMENTS—Length, 43 inches. Height, 27 inches.

SPECIFICATIONS—All steel construction. Designed in imitation of modern war machine. Dummy machine gun swivels horizontally and vertically and has a clicking device which is operated by turning a wire handle. Back axle runs on ball bearings.

FINISH—Body stove enamelled in green. Mudguards enamelled black.

EQUIPMENT—Crank drive. Cast steering wheel. Head lights. Number plate.

WHEELS—9 inch stamped steel spoke with ⅜ inch rubber tyres, enamelled to match body. Large nickel plated hub caps.

Weight, 43 lbs.

SPARE PARTS ALWAYS OBTAINABLE
10

The above pages from the 1941 Cyclops catalogue give a good indication of just how varied their pedal cars had become.
It also included a fabulous montage of the factory workings at Leichhardt (top left).

TRICYCLES Nos. 18, 19 and 20

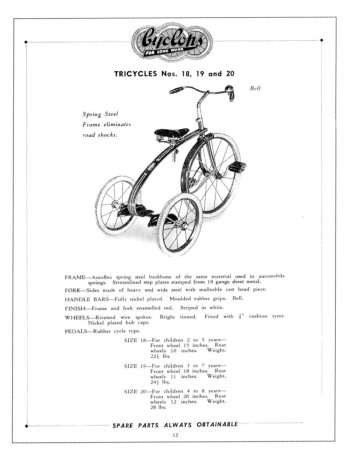

Bell

Spring Steel Frame eliminates road shocks.

FRAME—Autoflex spring steel backbone of the same material used in automobile springs. Streamlined step plates stamped from 18 gauge sheet metal.

FORK—Sides made of heavy and wide steel with malleable cast head piece.

HANDLE BARS—Fully nickel plated. Moulded rubber grips. Bell.

FINISH—Frame and fork enamelled red. Striped in white.

WHEELS—Rivetted wire spokes. Bright tinned. Fitted with ⅞″ cushion tyres. Nickel plated hub caps.

PEDALS—Rubber cycle type.

SIZE 18—For children 2 to 5 years— Front wheel 15 inches. Rear wheels 10 inches. Weight, 22½ lbs.

SIZE 19—For children 3 to 7 years— Front wheel 18 inches. Rear wheels 11 inches. Weight, 24½ lbs.

SIZE 20—For children 4 to 8 years— Front wheel 20 inches. Rear wheels 12 inches. Weight, 26 lbs.

SPARE PARTS ALWAYS OBTAINABLE

12

THE CYCLOPS SIDECAR

Bell

MEASUREMENTS—Length overall, 39 inches. Width overall, 22 inches. Height, 27 inches.

FRAME AND FORK—Made of heavy and wide steel.

SIDECAR AND MUDGUARDS—Stamped from 24 gauge first quality sheet steel.

HANDLE BARS—Fully nickel plated. Moulded rubber grips.

FINISH—Stove enamelled in red. Striped in white.

WHEELS—Nickel plated hubs. Rustless steel cycle spokes. Fitted with ⅞ inch cushion tyres. Front wheel 15 inches. Back wheels 10 inches.

PEDALS—Rubber. Ball-bearing.

EQUIPMENT—Nickel plated hub caps. Tail light. Bell.

Weight, 30 lbs.

SPARE PARTS ALWAYS OBTAINABLE

17

CYCLOPS DINKIE
(Regd.)
No. 8

(For children 3 to 6 years)

SPECIFICATIONS—Heavy steel frame and fork. Wooden seat with metal skirt. Streamlined mudguard over front wheel. Rubber handle grips. Tail light.

FRONT WHEEL—9 inch reinforced disc with ½ inch rubber tyre. Rubber pedals.

REAR WHEELS—7 inch reinforced disc with ½ inch rubber tyre. Nickel plated hub caps.

FINISH — Stove enamelled in red. Striped in white. Weight, 15½ lbs.

DINKIE EXPRESS

(For children 2 to 5 years)

SPECIFICATIONS—Frame, fork, seat and tray all made of heavy gauge steel. Rubber handle grips. Tray— 12 x 11 inches, 2½ inches deep.

FRONT WHEEL—8 inch reinforced disc with ½ inch rubber tyre. Rubber pedals.

REAR WHEELS—6 inch reinforced disc with ½ inch rubber tyres. Nickel plated hub caps.

FINISH — Frame, fork and wheels stove enamelled in green. Seat and tray enamelled cream. Weight, 12½ lbs.

SPARE PARTS ALWAYS OBTAINABLE

19

SMALL TOYS

Lines illustrated on this page and the one following comprise our Small Toy range as apart from our Children's Vehicles. Minimum quantity procurable of any one line—¼ dozen.

TIN HAT

A Scale model of the regulation army equipment. Stamped from 28 gauge motor body sheet. Elastic chin strap.

FINISH—Stove enamelled khaki brown.

THE "BIZZIE-BEE" CARPET SWEEPER

SPECIFICATIONS — Body stamped from sheet steel. Wooden handle and wheels. Brush made of first quality bristles on wire spindle.

MEASUREMENTS — Length overall, 30 inches. Body, 7½ x 5½ inches.

FINISH — Body enamelled cream, handle blue.

WAGGON No. 0

SPECIFICATIONS—Stamped from first quality steel. Tray— 13½ x 7½ inches, 2 inches deep. WHEELS—3 inch disc with imitation tyre. FINISH—Enamelled in red.

SPARE PARTS ALWAYS OBTAINABLE

31

Four more pages from the 1941 catalogue—showcasing the new tricycles and Dinkie, as well as the new waggon (bottom right) and small toys.

Mrs McGlashan and her 'first set of wheels';
Dinkie No. 4 (1940) sold for 13s 3d ($1.32).

All these marvellous toys were to disappear for a period of four years, mainly due to the shortage of materials—particularly the rubber needed for the tyres of the wheeled toys. What materials Cyclops *did* have were kept for the specially made Dinkies and tricycles that the firm was allowed to manufacture for institutions such as orphanages and hospitals. These were mainly used by victims of Infantile Paralysis (now known as Poliomyelitis), to strengthen and exercise their limbs. The only other production besides these toys and a small amount of defence work, was a limited number of full-size prams, all of which were under the strict rules and auspices of the War Organisation of Industry (W.O.I.).

The War Organisation of Industry was an all-powerful government department during the war years, especially after Japan had entered the war. This division of government bureaucracy closed down many toy manufacturing companies, virtually overnight in some instances. If a firm was permitted to manufacture, even in very limited quantities, they had to go before a board and obey very strict by-laws. The firm was only allowed to continue production after proving that they were only using up materials that were on hand, or were not necessary for war work; in particular, the firm had to prove that they were not employing men or women who could be better used in the manufacturing of much-needed war items—thus, a shortage of skilled labour became a very big obstacle.

Most of the machines used by Cyclops in the manufacture of wheeled toys were unable to be converted to war use, so from a workforce of 250–350 workers in 1941 (with about 100 personnel in the tricycle division and about 200 in the various other wheeled toy areas), the company's manpower was reduced to about 85 employees. They were mainly occupied with making full-sized baby prams and strollers and a few items for defence. Manufacturing was now entirely under the guidance of W.O.I, and it was only the prams and strollers, the occasional special order of tricycles for use in institutions, and the small war defence contracts that kept the factory from being closed down completely.

On one occasion Mr. E. Heine of Cyclops appeared before the W. O. I. and enquired whether he would be able to use some of the materials on hand to manufacture a few scooters. This idea was squashed by typical bureaucratic reasoning—W.O.I. stated that a child riding a scooter would use one leg more than the other, and this could lead to complications. (Apparently they never realised that if a child's leg got tired when he/she rode a scooter, the child had enough sense to automatically switch to the other leg, thus exercising both legs.) I still retain very fond memories of many excursions on my beloved No. 3 DeLuxe Scooter in the early 1940s; the tumbles that were had by myself and my friends through carelessness when travelling down what then seemed a rather steep hill—what's more, none of us ever suffered any lasting ill effects from our childhood activities.

Even in 1944, Mr. Ernest Heine had to front up, along with Mr. Scott (the head of Peerless Toys)—between them, these men headed the two largest wheeled toy manufacturing plants in Australia at that time—to the W.O.I. and ask whether a few tons of rubber (for rubber tyres) could not be made available for them to enable the manufacture of their very limited range of items to continue.

A beautifully restored Cyclops 'Chevrolet'; this model was popular in 1940, 1941 and even after the war. The design was altered in the early 1950s and the new shape became known as the Comet in 1953.

4

POST-WAR YEARS 1946—
THE GIANT ARISES

It was not until November 1946 (over thirty years after Heine originally began his manufacturing), that the firm now known as Cyclops Pty Ltd returned to peacetime production. Cyclops attempted to start filling the very large void caused by the shortage of toys during the war years with the manufacture of a Dinkie model, and 'Tricycle No. 12' (this was later renamed 'Tricycle 212'). Both these models were distributed on a quota system and were sold to the general public under strict governmental price control. One class of baby carriage and a wooden-framed stroller (long since discontinued), also featured in the company's initial post-war production. Many of the early 1940–41 prototype wheeled toys were gradually re-introduced, particularly the popular Dinkie and scooter lines.

The pedal cars followed the guidelines that Cyclops Pty Ltd had set in the years before—they mirrored in form (where possible), the shape of the cars commonly seen on the street; so their famous pedal cars once again changed to a more modern shape and examples of these were well in vogue by the middle of the 1950s.

Many thanks are here extended to Ross Schmidt of WA, who has kindly sent me information on Cyclops over the years and through his copious copies of old advertising material I am able to fill in some of the gaps in the company's late 1940s production of wheeled toys.

In 1948 the *Broadcaster* contained an advertisement for Elliotts, advertising a Cyclops scooter that was available in green and orange with stand and brake for the sum of £2 ($4.00).

The Myer Emporium in Melbourne advertised in 1948 that you could layby a Cyclops Dinkie trike, 'Waggon No. 0', 'Tricycle No. 12', and a wooden pram—ready for Christmas.

Bairds of Western Australia advertised in their Winter catalogue of 1949, that they had a Cyclops scooter for sale. The *West Australian*, in their issue of November 23 1949, advertised three different sized Cyclops scooters available at £1 5s, £2 4s 6d and £3 17s 6d, ($2.50, $4.45 and $7.75 respectively).

By the time Bairds' Christmas catalogue for 1949–50 was ready for release, the list of available Cyclops toys had grown considerably and now included a metal doll's pram and a strollette, both similar to those manufactured in the early 1940s. There was also an 'Express Waggon', 'Dinkie Express' and 'DeLuxe' scooter, as well as the ever-popular 'No. 3 Scooter', the 'Tricycle No. 2', No. 12, and the 'Super DeLuxe' model. More significant is the evidence of what may have been the first production of pedal cars after the war—the 'Chevrolet' pedal car; it was similar in lines to their 1941 model.

Examples of these now-famous and eminently collectable metal pedal cars manufactured from 1950 through to the 1970s can be found in the Collector's Guide (page 71). The listing includes important details and relevant particulars of these valuable toys.

Home repaired example of Tricycle No. 12—Cyclops toys go on forever

A lovely old hand car or trolley car, introduced in the early 1920s (the wheels on this example may not be original).

Cyclops bicycle, manufactured in two sizes and advertised in 1924.

A 1920s vintage Cyclops tricycle, as shown in the 1924 catalogue (Courtesy Beryl Seargent, N.S.W.)

This lovingly restored Cyclops 'Chrysler' pedal car was advertised in the 1938 and 1941 Cyclops catalogues

Two children enjoy a spin in a Cyclops two-seater 'Packard' from the 1930s.

Beautifully restored by Gary Jones, this Cyclops 'Dodge' pedal car was produced between 1935 and 1938.

The Cyclops No. 4 Dinkie was first advertised in 1932 and proved to be very popular.

A Cyclops 'Chrysler' pedal car in the process of being restored by Peter Christensen, Brisbane.

A fine example of a Cyclops tricycle with an autoflex spring steel backbone, made in 1940 and reissued after WW II.

First introduced as the Cyclops Tricycle No. 12 in 1938, this was one of the first wheeled toys produced by Cyclops after WW II. It was later re-named No. 212.

Aaron Gee, sitting in his 1940s Cyclops 'Chevrolet', restored by grandfather Phillip Ross.

Nev and younger brother Kevin in trike and sidecar, circa 1945 (Courtesy Nev Dixon, QLD)

Nev's Cyclops trike and sidecar from 1945—fifty years of play and still in one piece (Courtesy Nev Dixon, QLD)

An early 1940s Cyclops truck (Courtesy Nev Dixon, QLD).

Cyclops 'Lightning' pedal car, restored by Gary Jones

Table Walker doll produced by Moldex of Melbourne.

'Nursery Rhyme Super Tea Set' in plastic—another Moldex product

An unusual Moldex toy—the kangaroo jumps when the rubber bulb at the end of the tube is squeezed

A range of Pedigree Dolls—also produced by Moldex
(Courtesy Australasian Sportsgoods and Toy Retailer)

Two young owners discuss the finer points of their 1950 'Ford Clipper' pedal cars—the 'Ford' name was later dropped. (Courtesy of the A.M. Australian Magazine, *December 1950)*

Rescued from a rubbish dump, this 1950s Cyclops 'Comet' is the pride and joy of Mark Van Eck.

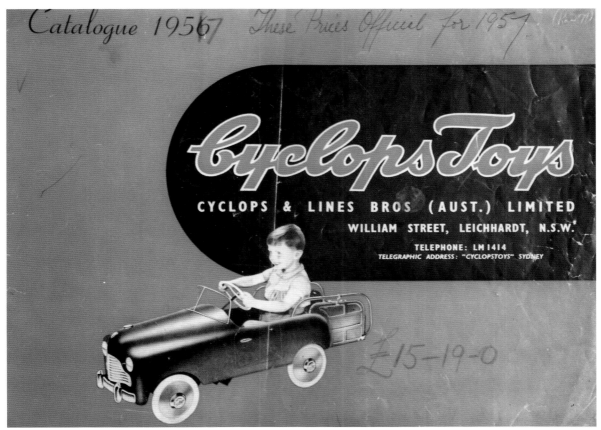

Cover of the 1956 Cyclops & Lines Bros catalogue

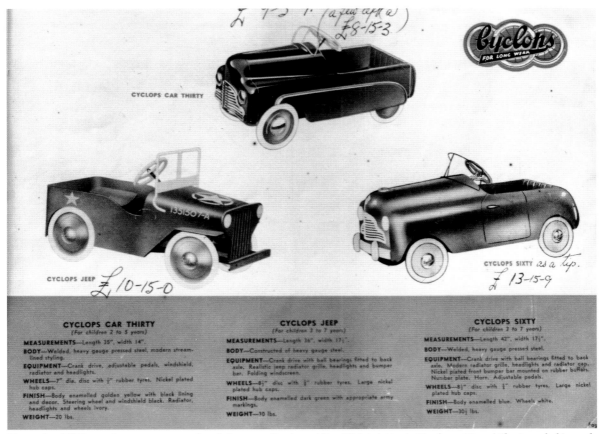

From the 1956 catalogue, a page of pedal cars—Cyclops 'Car Thirty' (top), Cyclops 'Jeep' (bottom left), and Cyclops 'Sixty' (bottom right).

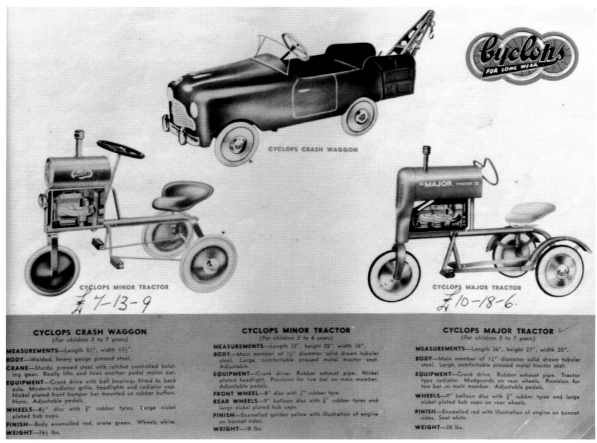

From the 1956 catalogue—the Crash Waggon (top), and (left and right) the 'Minor' and 'Major' tractors

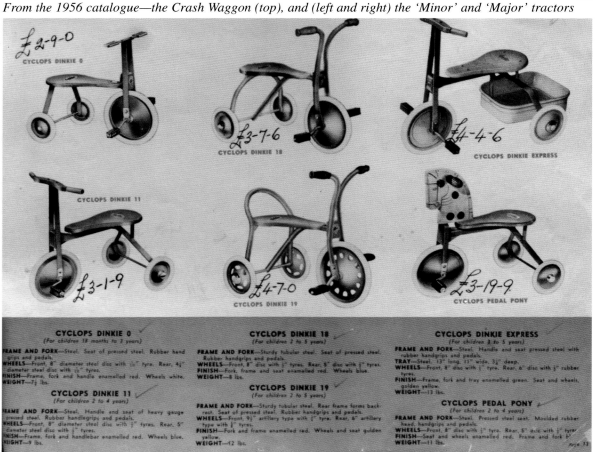

A range of Dinkies from 1956, including the Cyclops Pedal Pony (bottom right).

First introduced in 1953, the Cyclops 'Comet' is displayed at the Brisbane Motor Show, 1996

An early 1950s Cyclops 'Ford Clipper', before the brand name was dropped.

This colourful advertisement first appeared in the Australian Women's Weekly *in 1952—it has been re-issued as a postcard*

Restored 1956 'Clipper' pedal car—after the car had been redesigned and the name 'Ford' had been dropped.

Restored 1956 Crash Waggon (Courtesy Peter Christensen)

Cover of the 1957 Cyclops & Lines Bros catalogue

The cover of the 1959 Cyclops & Lines Bros catalogue showcases a variety of Australian wheeled toys.

The 1948 Myer toy promotion.

A post-war 'Chevrolet' pedal car with spoked wheels—a treasure in those days—shortages of materials meant toys had to be redesigned.

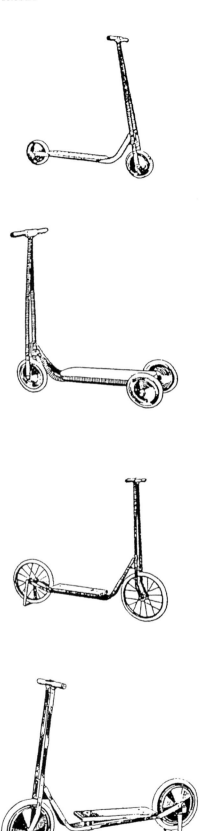

Scooter model nos 7, 6, 8 and 10—all were popular during the late 1940s

5

1950s—CHANGE IN THE AIR

Post-war growth both of turnover and production continued at a very rapid rate and this was helped by the import restrictions on toys that the Australian government had introduced just after the end of WW II. These restrictions limited the importing of toys that were manufactured by the large British firm of Lines Bros to about one-fifth of their former total.

It was apparently in 1950 that the new streamlined Cyclops 'Ford Clipper' pedal car first came on the scene; it was advertised along with the 'Chevrolet' pedal car in a Bairds catalogue. In August 1950 Myer of Melbourne advertised that an all-steel Dinkie was available for the price of £1 15s 3d ($3.52) and a steel-framed Cyclops scooter cost £3 9s 3d ($6.92).

The 1950–51 catalogue by Bairds of Western Australia listed the following wheeled toys by Cyclops: dolls' strollettes, dolls' prams, Tricycles No. 2 and No. 12, as well as the 'DeLuxe Tricycle', Cyclops 'Dinkie No. 5', the Cyclops 'Dinkie Express', and the Cyclops 'Chevrolet' pedal car which sold for £5 7s 9d ($10.78).

Baird's 1951–52 catalogue included the Cyclops 'Ford Clipper' pedal car and the new model of the 'Chevrolet' pedal car, as well as the Express Waggons, the 'Dinkie Express' and 'DeLuxe Scooter', plus the strollettes and prams. A later 1952 catalogue listed the 'Clipper' and 'Chevrolet' pedal cars (this appears to have been the last year of production of the 'Chevrolet'), Dinkies, the 'Dinkie Express', Tricycles No. 2, 12, 18 and 20 and Scooters No. 3, 5 and 10. It also included dolls' prams, strollettes and the new Nibs Chariot, (a folding stroller for dolls).

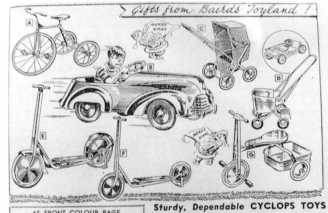

A page from the later 1952 Bairds' catalogue (for Christmas); the car pictured is the Clipper; the Nibs Chariot is illustrated (centre, right), above the Dinkie (Courtesy Ross Schmidt)

The year 1953 saw the introduction of the 'Comet' pedal car; other products available during the later part of that year were the 'Clipper' car (the name Ford had been dropped), Cyclops Scooters No. 3, 5 and 10, Tricycles No. 2 (the old No. 12), 220 and 420. Dinkies—including 'Dinkie No. 5' and the 'Dinkie Express'—also made an appearance, as did Doll's Pram No. 1 and the Doll's Nibs Chariot.

Two more cars were listed in 1954—the 'Tip Truck' and the 'Station Waggon', along with the 'Comet', Cyclops 'Sixty' and the 'Clipper'. This brought the total number of pedal cars being produced to five, and these were complemented by the still-popular Flivver. 'Pram No. 24', a rigid frame tricycle, and a tricycle with an autoflex spring steel backbone were also introduced in 1954 and 'Scooter No. 6' was reintroduced.

The first year of production and sale for the Cyclops 'Jeep' and 'Tractor' was 1955. Many of the 120 large metal presses were kept busy turning out the various metal components needed in the manufacture of the six pedal cars, namely the Cyclops 'Clipper', Cyclops 'Sixty', Cyclops 'Station Waggon', Cyclops 'Comet', Cyclops 'Jeep' and Cyclops 'Tip Truck'. These were all shown in the 1955 catalogue, where it was clear they were produced in a much more modern style than their 1941 counterparts.

Having an original 1956 Cyclops catalogue in my possession, I can give you the full scope of their proposed production for that year. There were ten pedal cars in their range, colourfully named as follows:

Youngster imitating his elders under a 1950 Ford Clipper; stylistic similarities between the adult car and the child's one is obvious (Reproduced by courtesy of the A.M. Australian Magazine *December 1950*)

Youngster Gary 'Pedal Car Pusher' Jones in his trusty Cyclops car.

Page from The Retailer *of 1952, announcing the new business arrangement to the trade.*

'Comet'
'Dart'
'Tip Truck'
'Car Thirty'
'Jeep'
'Sixty'
'Jupiter'
'Clipper'
'Station Waggon'
'Crash Waggon'

There were also two tractors—the Major and the Minor; the Flivver was still a favourite as well. The tricycle range included the nos 212, 220, 310, 400, 900, 800, 800T, 'Bin Trike 216B' and 'Bin Trike 820B'; in addition, there were Nos 112 and 116 and the chain-drive tricycle, the 'Jet Motorcycle', 'Cyclobike' and the Cyclops 'Trailer'. The Dinkie range included Dinkies No. 0, 11, 18 and 19, the 'Dinkie Express' and the revised design of the 'Pedal Pony', a beloved favourite with children.

The scooter range included nos 3, 5, 6, 16 and 17. The range of dolls' prams that were available had grown to incorporate nos 16, 20 and 24, folding pram 20B and 24B, 'Doll's Nibs Chariot No. 1' and No. 2, and the hooded version No. 2H. Three different kinds of

wheelbarrows were available, plus three styles of waggon, a nursery rocker, the 'Bizzie-Bee Carpet Sweeper', 'Lawnmower No. 1' and a set of garden tools.

Along with the increased post-war production came the threat of a take-over. The large British firm of Lines Bros (also manufacturers of wheeled toys), had been keen to have shares in this Australian toy giant even before the outbreak of war in 1939. With the import restrictions on their toys in the 1950s, the UK company's desire to manufacture their range of toys here in Australia was even greater and they wished to either set up or buy factories in Australia, as they had already done in New Zealand in 1946 and Canada in 1947.

In 1951 Lines Bros finally succeeded in their project; they acquired a 49% interest in the original Australian company of Cyclops Pty Ltd, which until then had been owned by the E. J. Heine organisation. Ernest J. Heine was the son of John Heine, the founder of Cyclops. Mr Heine Senior had for many years assiduously fought off any amalgamation with the large British company. By 1955 Lines Bros had acquired the remaining 51% of the Cyclops company shares, to become Cyclops & Lines Bros (Aust.) Ltd, with Ernest J. Heine holding the position of Director in the new company.

Bryan Baker on his 1950s Cyclops Dinkie

From 1951 to 1955 Cyclops and Lines Bros (Aust.) Ltd was in fact a company listed on the Australian Stock Exchange. Lines Bros Ltd owned 40% of the shares, the Heine family owned 40%, and the Australian Public, 20%.

In the early 1950s, several men joined the firm and had a profound effect on Cyclops. One was Bill Hamp-Adams, who joined the firm in 1951 and later became their modelmaker and designer. Among the cars he designed were the 'Jeep', the 'Lightning' and the Major and Minor Tractors; in the small toy range, Bill was responsible for the toy 'Victa Mower' and all the plastic toys until his retirement in 1982.

Another man who joined Cyclops in the 1950s was Wally Cray, who from 1954 onwards had many years with Cyclops and was to become their Works Director. He was also with the firm during the time of its expansion and take-overs; he retired in 1988.

Throughout the 1950s the merged company Cyclops & Lines Bros (Aust.) Limited consistently introduced new lines to their growing range of wheeled toys According to their well illustrated 1959 catalogue, they were producing twelve varieties of pedal cars, including the popular 'Dart', 'Prince' and 'Comet' (at the bottom of the range), through to the 'Tip Truck', 'Super Scooper', 'Lightning' and 'Jeep'; at the higher end of the price range was the 'Fire Engine Jeep', 'Sixty-Tip', 'Radio Taxi', 'Jupiter' and 'Station Waggon'. The last three sold for over £15 ($30.00) each—not that much less than the average weekly working-class wage at the time. Two other pedal-powered vehicles were the Major and Minor Tractors. There were also fourteen tricycles, ranging in price from below £5 ($10.00), to a very elaborate chain-driven model selling at over £22 ($44.00); a trailer for use behind the tricycles was also available. There were two bicycles in the range and a 'Trietta' pedal scooter, (a definite sign of the times).

Eight Dinkies including the 'Jupiter Rocket' (with a main frame that resembled a plane), and six scooters including the still popular No. 3 (which had been in production since the 1930s), also featured in the catalogue. There were also eight dolls' prams manufactured in metal and models in folding leathercloth, as well as four dolls' strollers—including one for twin dolls. Four wheelbarrows (one of which came complete with garden tools), were also available, along with four waggons, five rockers—two with horses—and the wonderful 'Pegusus Trotting Gig'.

Amongst what could be called the miscellaneous items were a rotary mower, a lawnmower with sets of garden tools; a range of eleven welded steel pushalong trucks, a large 'Dockside Crane', two 'Shopping Jeeps' (or trolleys), one doll's swing, a doll's highchair, a Cyclops 'See-Saw' roundabout, a nursery wading pool, a combination desk/chair set and a table and chair set were also hallmarks of 1959. A considerable increase in production and diversity was evident during the decade.

The Senior Management team during the expansionary period from 1955 to 1971 was as follows:

Ronald R. Dunk	Chairman & Managing Director
Kenneth F. Chapman	Financial Director/Director of All Subsidiaries
Walter V. Cray	Works Director
David W. Grant	Sales and Marketing Director

The former Managing Director of Cyclops, Mr Ernest Heine, in 1958. (Courtesy The Retailer)

The Managing Director of Cyclops & Lines Bros, Mr Ron Dunk, in 1958. (Courtesy The Retailer)

Left: *The Wheel Manufacturing department for Cyclops toys at Leichhardt*

Right: *Outside view of the Cyclops manufacturing plant at Leichhardt during the 1950s*

Left: *Women at their sewing machines in the Soft Goods department of the Cyclops factory*

Left: *Final assembly of some of the Cyclops wheeled toys*

Right: *Some of the presses at the factory*

Left: *Mass production of pedal cars; 20, 000 of these cars were produced in 1950. The steel car bodies were spray painted with red enamel (see the spray booth to the right), hung on racks and placed in drying ovens where they were baked at 200° F.*

As Cyclops, which had its large premises at Leichhardt in Sydney, were primarily manufacturers of pressed metal wheeled toys and Lines Bros badly needed a factory (a plastics manufacturing set-up in particular) where they could manufacture their English-made lines such as 'Pedigree Dolls', 'Tri-ang Railways' and 'Scalextric' racing cars, Lines Bros looked at Melbourne as a likely location. The UK giant hoped to combine the manufacture of these plastic-related goods with a warehouse in which to store the Cyclops lines, instead of paying for storage in a separate situation. Such a set-up would also prevent Lines Bros from suffering the high import duties and sales taxes then in force.

Lines Bros found a suitable factory situated in Fairfield, a suburb of Melbourne; it was owned by Moldex Ltd, which fortunately for Lines Bros was undergoing financial problems. Moldex instigated the purchase in December 1956. The factory had a floor space of over 65, 000 sq. ft and four acres of land. Lines Bros being able to purchase all the Ordinary Shares of Moldex Ltd, the actual acquisition date was 1 March 1957.

Moldex had been founded on the post-war theory that anything could be produced in plastic. All its products were made of plastic and included extruded hose pipes, plastic sanitary bins, washing up basins, combs and toys. Dolls manufactured in hard plastic are still found with the winged 'M' logo of Moldex, but it is not known whether these dolls were made by Moldex before or after the Lines Bros purchase of the factory.

Moldex had installed a fair amount of very expensive machinery that enabled them to manufacture plastics in the various ways; injection, extrusion, thermo-setting, vacuum, etc. Along with the largest injection-moulding machine in the southern hemisphere (at the time), there was also a fully equipped tool and die shop and a great deal of plant—just what Lines Bros needed for their plastic division under the auspices of Cyclops & Lines Bros.

After some re-organisation at the Moldex factory, they were soon able to manufacture 'Pedigree Dolls' using imported dies. This was done under the 'Pedigree Moldex' label. The toy giant was also responsible for the manufacture of Tri-ang Railways with an Australian flavour; some of these products were later produced in the livery colours of various Australian state railways. All the components necessary for the manufacture of 'Scalextric' Raceways, then sold in Australia, were later produced in the Moldex factory in Melbourne.

The first dolls produced were injection-moulded, including the heads. Moulds were brought from England and loaned between Australia, New Zealand and South Africa—this is why you sometimes find dolls marked with abbreviations of these countries. Although the hard plastic used in these dolls was referred to as 'cellulose acetate' by the parent company and in the Australian advertising campaigns, the actual material used in this type of hard plastic doll is acrylic in origin, and should have been referred to as methylmethacrylate, or hard plastic. Where hair was needed to enhance a doll's appearance, a sewn wig was glued onto the scalp. Dolls of this kind came in non-walking and walking versions, with the best selling doll being a 22" (56 cm) walking model. It was sold under the model code AW22/0/WS in its undressed form.

In a letter from David Grant (formerly of Cyclops & Lines Bros) that I received in 1986, he explained that many thousands of dolls were manufactured in sizes ranging from 10" (25½ cm) to 22" (56 cm). Most of the dolls were made by the 'blow-moulding' method of manufacture; in simple terms, this meant that a hot, soft tube of plastic was gravity-fed into an open two-sided mould, which was then closed. Air was injected from below to blow the plastic outward into the shape of the mould. The whole process was timed to cool and be

The Moldex factory in Fairfield, Melbourne—the winged 'M' logo is prominently displayed

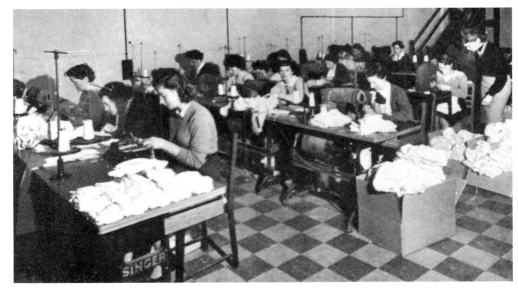

The Moldex factory at work in the 1950s, and two of the finished products in 1958. The largest injection-moulding machine in Australia was at the factory (top left), along with the only rotary self-contained moulding machine in the country (top right).

opened for the removal of the moulded body, limbs, etc. The stage was now set for an even greater titan in the blossoming Australian toy industry.

Also in production was a range of 'Pedigree Playtime Pets'—a collection of vinyl toys, mischievous and engaging, soft and hygienic with a built-in whistle. The range included the following designs: A181 Fish called 'Tiddler', A182 Puppy ('Pup'), A183 Dog with Boot named 'Mischief', A184 Lamb or 'Lambkin', A185 Cat ('Kitty'), A187 Dog known as 'Woofie', A189 'Ducky' and A190 'Jumbo'.

The manufacture of Tri-ang Railways at the Moldex plant was also expanded in the form of their '00' range with a typical Australian layout and a brilliant streamlined version of the famous Victorian Diesel Express. The range also included a Transcontinental Goods set and later a Sydney suburban electric train set, all of which were moulded from Lustrex Hi-Test 88 plastic supplied by Monsanto Chemicals Ltd. Using this material, intricate shapes and fine detail could be reproduced with a smooth lustrous surface finish in the required colour. Eveready Batteries also advised Cyclops & Lines Bros that they had designed and marketed throughout Australia, a special

4½ volt (No. 714) dry cell for the operation of the Melbourne-manufactured Tri-ang Railways.

Once Poly Vinyl Chloride (PVC or vinyl) became available, hair could be sewn into the head (inrooting) of a doll. By the end of the 1950s some of the dolls were being manufactured from this new type of plastic, and by the latter part of the 1960s vinyl had become the accepted doll medium. This next generation of dolls were all cast of vinyl, using a rotation method of manufacture. The vinyl materials for this type of doll came in a thick liquid form; this was poured into the mould attached, with many others, to a large frame. The frame was revolved and tumbled so as to 'throw' the liquid vinyl to the extremities of the mould. Once this was done, the vinyl could be cooled and pulled from the mould.

The first product was AV10S/G, meaning a 10" vinyl doll with straight legs and a moulded head. The best sellers were AV16SW/0—the numerals were used to indicate dressed versions of the dolls: for example, AV16SW/5. Vinyl dolls with moving limbs were later manufactured with blow-moulded bodies to reduce the weight of the doll.

*Advertisement for the Tri-ang Transcontinental Goods set with a 'typical' Australian layout; the set was made at the Moldex factory. (*Courtesy* The Retailer)*

From the late 1950s (approximately 1956/57)—the Pegasus Trotting Gig, with Ron Chant in his silks, ready for a race!

By 1959 Cyclops & Lines Bros were impressing both the trade and the general public with the production of their all-vinyl Pedigree walking doll—the very first vinyl walking doll. She had rooted saran hair and sleeping eyes; the doll retailed at £2 9d ($4.10) for the 11" (26 cm) size and £3 5s 6d ($6.55) for the 16" (41 cm) version. The average man's wage at this time was just a little over £20 ($40.00) per week, so the toy would have been quite a treat.

By this time, other toys such as the toughened Tri-ang vinyl ride-on pushalong toys, had been introduced. This range included a friendly-looking elephant, bears, dogs and a horse. Their retail prices ranged from £8 ($16.00) to £10 ($20.00).

Besides the normal Cyclops metal pedal car range of the era, boys were being catered for during 1959 with the very newest idea in pedal cars. The car, a superbly designed child-sized M.G. racing car, was manufactured with a fibreglass body (the first one of its kind made in Australia). It was introduced by Cyclops, as the company had employed their own designer and model maker—Bill Hamp-Adams; as always, Cyclops continued to carry out their belief in moving with the times, both in the styling of the product and their use of materials. With this car Cyclops entered a new era in wheeled toys—The Plastic Age. Unfortunately, unlike their metallic grandparents, many of the later plastic models haven't stood the test of time. This is mainly due to Australia's harsh climate and the effect of ultra violet rays on plastic.

A 1957 Cyclops Tipper pedal car, with Joy Toys' Golliwog and dog as drivers, and Pedigree doll beside Joy Toy bear, riding in the tray. (Photograph taken in Panaroo's Playthings Doll and Toy Museum, 1980)

6

1960s ACQUISITIONS—
THE ZENITH OF ITS GROWTH

The wonderful years of the 1960s brought a wide variety of distinctively rugged, yet reliable toys to the public from the factories of the Cyclops/Moldex and Cyclops & Lines Bros (Aust.) Ltd group of companies. The upheavals and reorganisation that took place in this era while Cyclops managed to survive proved that a good product is the rock on which a sound business is built.

These were the years when the company expanded even further with take-overs of, or partnerships with, other toy manufacturing businesses; the famous Australian teddy bear manufacturer—Joy Toys—was one of these, as was Pilgrim. The latter's 'Hi-Speed' wheeled toys were often manufactured along the same lines as the Cyclops & Lines Bros products. The acquisition of Daymond

Early 1960s Cyclops 'Ranch Waggon', driven by Sandra Mazoudier.

Nostalgia was the theme for the 1960 catalogue—a ghostly old pedal car rides beside its modern counterpart.

Scalextric racing car sets—a very popular Cyclops line

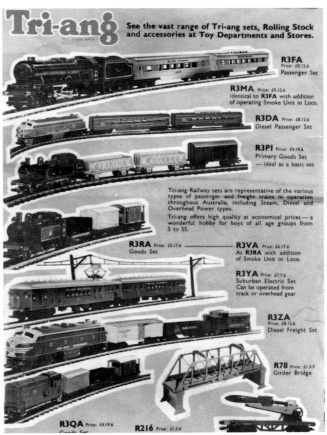

Tri-ang train sets—also popular and a consistent winner

A grand selection of life-like Pedigree dolls, including some of their celebrated bridal dolls.

'Rags' Nielson tries out a 1959/1960 Cyclops scooter.

Boys' Toy of the Year Award 1968 IN ENGLAND.

no strings

no wires

MOON PROBE

JOHNNY ASTRO

unique free-flight controlled space age toy!

The variable speed jet stream lifts the space vehicle off the launching pad, guides it up, sideways, down, to land on the simulated moon surface. Winner of the 1968 Boy's Toy of the Year Award in England, Johnny Astro is an absorbing toy — completely safe, operates on batteries or from a 12v transformer if used in conjunction with power conversion kit. Space vehicle is controlled solely by the jet stream which can be varied for speed and direction. Available at toy shops everywhere.

Boys' Toy of the Year in the UK in 1968—Johnny Astro

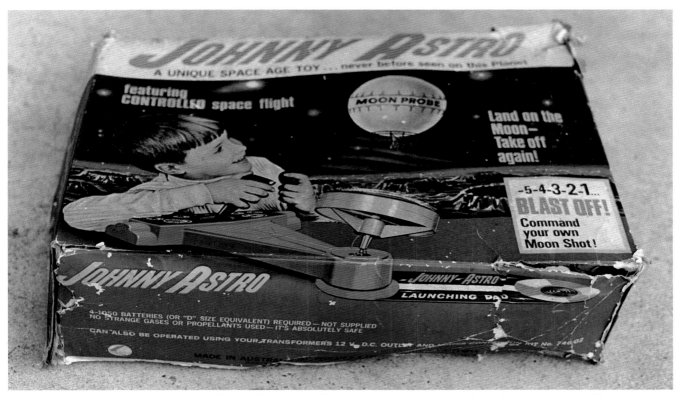

Space exploration was big news in the late 1960s, as was this unique Cyclops toy (made under licence by Moldex).

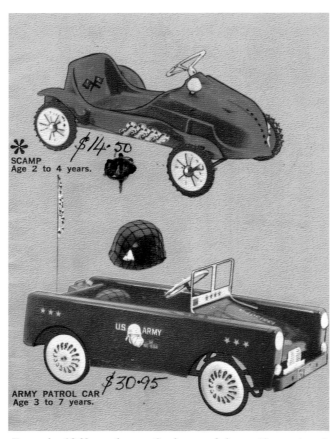

From the 1968 catalogue, Cyclops pedal cars 'Scamp' and 'Army Patrol' Car

New in 1967—Gyro-ring and the 'K. C. Jones' pullalong, a certain winner. (Courtesy Australasian Sportsgoods and Toy Retailer)

One of the most popular designs, this metal framed pram was on the market for many years.

CYCLOPS DOLL'S PRAM 16:

Weight 5 lbs. Sheet steel body 16" long, plated round steel handle, washable plastic hood and storm cover, wheels 5½" with ⅜" tyre, body emamelled pink with blue decorative trim, wheels and undergear white.

CYCLOPS DOLL'S PRAM 20:

Weight 11 lbs. Modern design sheet steel body 20" long, plated steel handle with washable plastic handgrip, plastic hood and storm cover, 6½" wheels with ⅜" tyres and plated hub caps, enamelled in gloss colours; hood and stormcovers in contrasting colour to tone.

CYCLOPS DOLL PRAM 24:

Weight 14 lbs. Modern steel body 24" long with distinctive mouldings; tubular steel handle with white plastic grip; washable leathercloth hood and stormcover; chrome-plated hood stays, handle and hub caps; shackle suspension 8" wheels with ⅜" tyres; body enamelled in pastel colours with undercarriage and wheels white; folding handle for easy storage.
A really attractive model with de luxe features.

CYCLOPS DOLL'S FOLDER 20 B:

Weight 11 lbs. Leathercloth body 20" long, 9¾" wide, 6" deep, sturdy steel frame with easy folding action, wheels 5½" pressed steel with ⅜" rubber tyres and nickel-plated hub caps, frame and wheels enamelled white, embossed leathercloth covering in attractive colours to tone.

CYCLOPS DOLL'S PRAM 16:

CYCLOPS DOLL'S PRAM 24:

CYCLOPS DOLL'S FOLDER 20 B:

CYCLOPS DOLL'S PRAM 20:

A small selection of 1950s Cyclops dolls' prams.

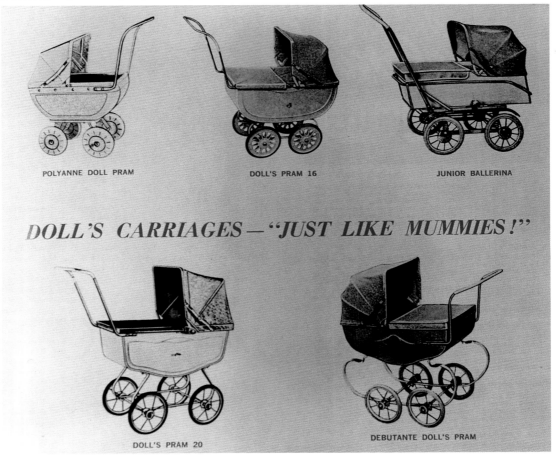

POLYANNE DOLL PRAM

DOLL'S PRAM 16

JUNIOR BALLERINA

DOLL'S CARRIAGES—"JUST LIKE MUMMIES!"

DOLL'S PRAM 20

DEBUTANTE DOLL'S PRAM

A decade on—a selection of 1960s Cyclops dolls' prams.

Above: *Cover of the 1961 Cyclops catalogue*

Below: *Pages from the 1963 catalogue, showing the new 'Junior' Motor Bike.*

Front cover of the 1963 Cyclops 50th anniversary catalogue.

These pages from the 1963 catalogue showcase the new line of playground toys.

The 1963 range of pedal cars, including the favourite 'Lightning' car.

From the anniversary catalogue—three new pedal cars, including the old-style 'Veteran' car (bottom left).

The diverse collection of tricycles in 1963 testifies to the imagination of the Cyclops designers; to the far right, centre, is the Tricycle '912 Tipper', and the tractor (far left, top) was a wonderful plaything for youngsters.

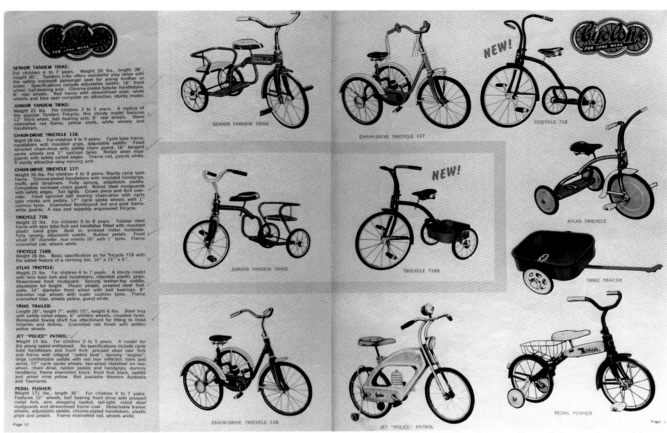

Cyclops trikes and two-wheelers in 1963; the wider selection of wheeled toys captures a larger slice of the market—older children can still enjoy Cyclops products.

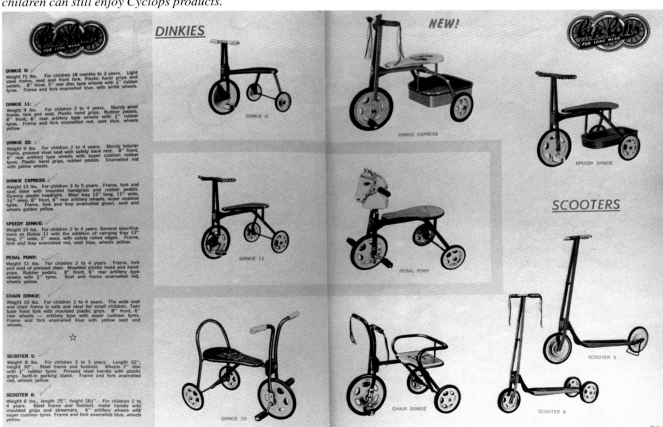

The 1963 collection of Cyclops Dinkies introduces the Dinkie Express.

Scooters and prams from the 1963 Cyclops catalogue.

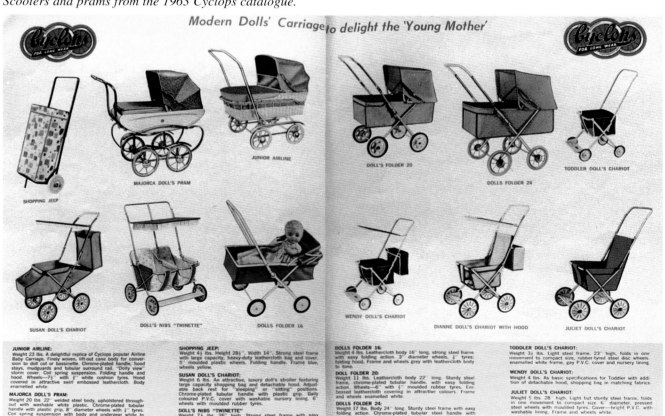

For the 'Young Mother'—Cyclops dolls' carriages from 1963.

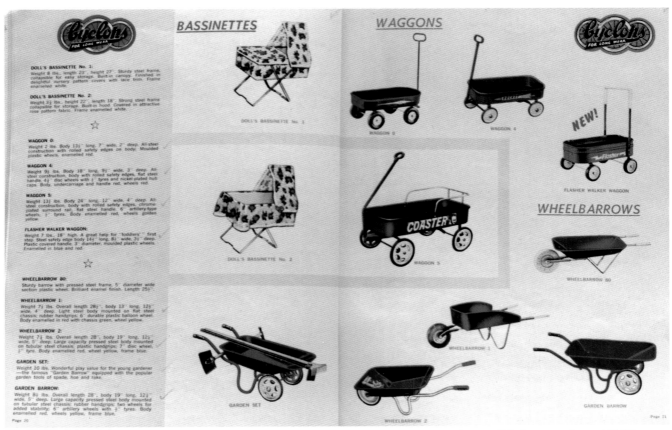

Brightly coloured bassinettes for baby dolls, wonderful waggons and wheelbarrows for small helpers outdoors (1963)

Cyclops pullalongs and nursery toys from the 1963 catalogue—at the bottom is the Cyclops guarantee that all their toys are 'enamelled with non toxic lead-free enamel'.

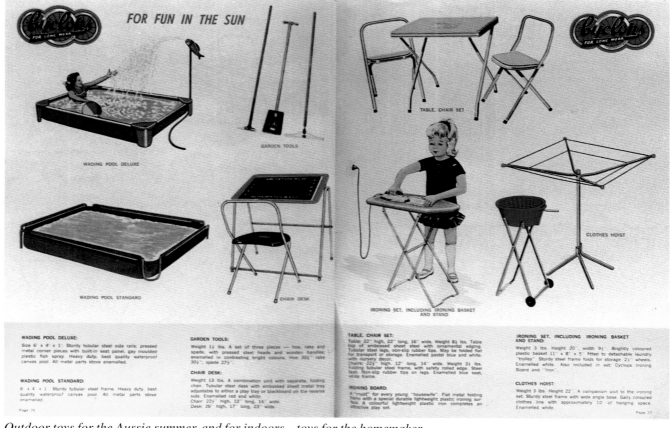

Outdoor toys for the Aussie summer, and for indoors—toys for the homemaker

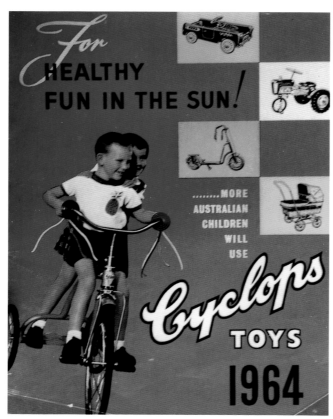

Front cover of the 1964 Cyclops catalogue

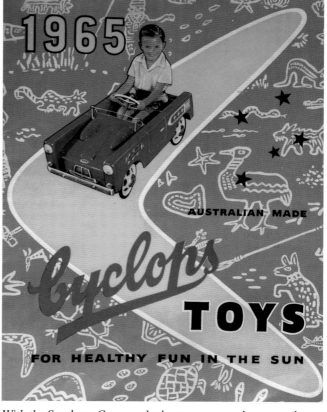

With the Southern Cross and a boomerang on the cover, the 1965 Cyclops catalogue proudly advertises 'Australian made'

A restored Cyclops 'Bermuda' pedal car from 1968 (Courtesy Peter Christensen)

As advertised in the 1963 catalogue—the Cyclops 'Veteran Car', restored and on display.

Front cover of the 1960 Pedigree Dolls catalogue, put out by Moldex, a subsidiary of Cyclops & Lines Bros.

Cover of the 1962 Pedigree Dolls catalogue by Moldex—bridal dolls were (and still are) popular with little girls.

The Pedigree 'Storybook of Dolls'

Winners of the 1965 Doll & Soft Toy Award (Courtesy The Retailer)

The new look 1964 Pedigree (Moldex) catalogue

A selection of Pedigree Dolls from 1965.

'Melody Dolls'—this new line from Pedigree was advertised in the 1968 Pedigree catalogue

A Cyclops Bin Trike from the 1960s.

A trio of Cyclops toys—a 1970s dolls' pram, a small two-wheeled scooter, and a pedal car with 'lace' wheels.

The striking front cover of the Cyclops 1971/72 toy catalogue

(used for making the large plastic components for some of the wheeled toys), which was claimed by the Australian makers to be the largest in the British Commonwealth (in 1964), the party went on to visit the company's new storehouse, where all four floors were 'chock-a-block' with cartons containing recently produced goods. This huge storage area allowed the company to store and stockpile the required amount of manufactured toys each year, ready for October, when the retail buyers wanted them for their Christmas market."

The new year was ushered in, and proved to be another celebratory experience for the company, with Cyclops & Lines Bros (Aust.) Ltd again managing to win several of the awards at the 1965 Toy of the Year Presentation:

After the presentation of the 'Toy of the Year' prize to Cyclops & Lines Bros for the Scalextric Set, the directors were questioned as to whether the Scalextric Set actually conformed to the conditions required for the prize; i.e. was the toy substantially Australian-made? Allegations were made that some of the major components were imported, (as they had at one time been for Lines Bros UK).

David Grant, then the Sales Director of Cyclops & Lines Bros, answered that of course the winning model was made in Australia; the motors were even wound on Australian-made components at their Moldex factory in Melbourne. The plastic car bodies, and also the straight and curved track were also manufactured in Melbourne, whilst the hand controllers were actually made by Cyclops.

The sceptics were later escorted around the Cyclops & Lines Bros Moldex factory at Fairfield in Melbourne, where they were not only able to see Scalextric sets being

David Grant (right), Sales Director of Cyclops & Lines Bros stands with the late Wally Cray, amongst the stacked goods ready for sale. (Courtesy The Retailer)

produced, but also the Tri-ang model railway sets and a large range of Pedigree dolls, 'Lifetime Toys' and other toys.

Joy Toys had produced some of their large range of soft toys under licence from Walt Disney and other American film producers over the years; such characters included 'Dorothy', 'Toto' and the 'Cowardly Lion' from the *Wizard of Oz* and 'Jimminy Cricket' from *Pinocchio*. So it was perfectly natural that in 1965 this renowned Australian name was permitted to produce a cloth 'Mary

Category	Award	Winner	Manufacturer
Toy of the Year	First Prize	Scalextric GP. 1 Set	Cyclops & Lines Bros (Moldex subsidiary)
Wheel Toy Section	First Prize	Fire Truck	Cyclops & Lines Bros
Soft Toy & Doll Section	First Prize	Pedigree Doll	Cyclops & Lines Bros (Moldex subsidiary)
Miscellaneous Section	First Prize	Tri-ang Train Set	Cyclops & Lines Bros (Moldex subsidiary)

The latest in the Tri-ang series—the Sydney 'Suburban Electric', designed to resemble the Sydney trains of the time. It was manufactured at the Moldex factory (Courtesy The Retailer, *October 1960)*

From The Retailer, *1967—'Footy' Dolls, in full V.F.L. club uniform of course. (Courtesy* The Retailer, *March 1967).*

New for 1968—the Cyclops & Lines Bros Eureka Cannon that really fired; the advertisemant appeared in the Australasian Sportsgoods and Toy Retailer

Poppins' doll at the height of the Disney film's popularity in Australia.

At the 1966 Melbourne Homes Exhibition, a full range of Cyclops wheeled toys were turned loose and an estimated 40, 000 children were given the freedom to ride, collide and display their prowess on a riding range adjacent to the Cyclops exhibit; the stand featured a full range of Cyclops products. At the opposite end of their exhibit was an additional area of excitement and attraction for children—a full display of Cyclops playground equipment. It included the new 'Ranger Tower', 'Lawn Swing' and 'Slide'. These were soon inundated with children of all ages, and Cyclops was delighted to see the affinity formed between children and the respective Cyclops toys.

Featured in the 1966 Australian Tri-ang Hornby model railway catalogue were: the 'Southern Aurora', the 'Trans Australia Express', the 'Interstate Freight Set' and the 'Suburban (Sydney) Set', plus a 'Diesel Freight Set', other rolling stock and accessories.

That lovable bear 'Winnie-the-Pooh', along with 'Piglet' and their friends, were made in 1967 under an exclusive franchise arrangement with Disney. They were included in the wonderful range of plush animals manufactured by Joy Toys, whose registered office and

showroom was situated at 70 Stephenson Street, Richmond in Melbourne.

Several action toys were introduced by Cyclops in 1967; these included the Cyclops 'Para-Launcher', complete with a skydiving parachutist who zoomed, (no skill required for this, according to the directions), about 100–150 ft (30–45 metres), into the air before the 'chute' opened and he returned to the ground. Another was the 'Gyro-Ring', a new ball game that was tipped to become the latest craze. 'Trik-Trak'—a battery-operated cross country road rally, which had an electric racing car, seven curves and two straight sections, a press-out bridge, a tunnel and a building—was also advertised extensively. Another battery-operated toy—the 'Big-Big Train' by Tri-ang—came complete with a 14" (35½ cm) 'Blue-Flyer' electric locomotive.

The year 1968 again brought accolades to Cyclops & Lines Bros at the Toy of the Year Awards; (see the table on page 51).

That year, the famous Australian racing car driver Leo Geohegan was asked to promote the Moldex Scalextric sets. Another promotion during 1968 involved the 'Melody Dolls'—a new line by Pedigree. These included the slim-bodied 16" (41 cm) 'Mandy', the 18" (46 cm) 'Bride Elizabeth', the 16" (41 cm) dark-complexioned

Category	Award	Winner		Manufacturer
Soft Toy Section	First Prize	A wonderful 18" (46 cm) Teddy Bear.		Joy Toys
Plastic Section	First Prize	'K.C Jones Train'; unusual 30" (76 cm) pushalong/pullalong floor train with a locomotive that tooted, and cars that either mooed or quacked when sqeezed.		Cyclops (Moldex)
Metal Section:	First Prize	'Wee Rocker'; the winning 'Wee Rocker' was the start of a special line for tiny tots.		Cyclops

'Bella', and the 16" (41 cm) 'Liz' and 'Sparky'. Besides these, a doll's hoist and laundry set were also displayed and promoted at the annual toy fair.

Not to be forgotten was the really imposing 'Eureka Cannon'. The canon measured about 30" (76 cm) in length, with wheels of 10½" (27 cm) diameter, and came with four harmless plastic cannon balls. The balls were manufactured in the company's plastic division. Also popular with the boys, was the Australian version of the 1968 English Toy of the Year—'Johnny Astro', (produced by Cyclops & Lines Bros). This educational toy was powered by a controllable air jet; The spaceship-like vehicle made landings on a plastic simulated moon-like crater base. It was described as a 'unique, free flight controlled, space-age toy which had no strings or wires'.

The range of Teacher pre-school toys was also expanded and the growing group of Lifetime Toys now included 'Table Cricket', 'Whirley Counter' (a counting frame), 'At Home Party Set' (a 32-piece party set vacuum-packed to the serving table included in the package), a 'Checklines Game' (pocket-sized), 'Flapper the Seal' (a pullalong/pushalong toy), and a simple plastic 'Whale and Pram' rattle. A large beach shovel, the 'Giant Beach Set' and a yacht (this came in a self-assembly kit), were wonderful extras for a trip to the beach.

In the games section could be found 'Play Bricks', 'Spell-it' (an educational word game) and 'Scatter Game', whilst 'Spirograph' and 'Spirotot' were manufactured under licence.

A 'Skippy' toy, representing the kangaroo star of the

The 'Big-Big' Train and Para-Launcher were made by Moldex (Courtesy Australasian Sportsgoods and Toy Retailer, September 1967).

This advertisement for Trik-Trak appeared in the Australasian Sportsgoods and Toy Retailer in October 1967.

'Li'l Miss Fussy'—A 1968 Cyclops & Lines Bros doll; she cried, wet her nappy and kicked her bedclothes off.

An extremely popular toy for girls, Mr Pierre Wigs was new in 1968.

Small toys produced under licence; the toy dog is from the Teacher line (Courtesy Australasian Sportsgoods and Toy Retailer)

Produced under licence in 1968, 'Baby Party' Doll was a big hit (Courtesy Australasian Sportsgoods and Toy Retailer, 1969).

popular children's television series *Skippy the Bush Kangaroo*, was manufactured in fur by the Morella company and sold through Cyclops & Lines Bros. The furry 'roo sold very well to both the lovers of the television series and Australia's overseas tourists.

In March 1969 the toy trade was notified that 'Cyclops & Lines Bros (Aust.) Ltd' would in future be known as 'Cyclops Tri-ang (Aust.) Ltd', and 'Moldex Ltd' would be known as 'Tri-ang Moldex (Aust.) Ltd'.

Cyclops Tri-ang were once more successful at the 1969 Toy of the Year Awards, with their successes detailed in the table below. A favourite, rather unusual toy for girls was introduced that year—the 'Mr. Pierre Wigs'. The wigs were produced in four different colours and came complete with rollers and a base. The wigs could be styled by their young owners into many different hairstyles.

Manufactured under the Pedigree label was a delightful 24" (61 cm) walking doll called 'Liza'. A 30" (76 cm) walking doll known as 'Laura' was also available, as was 'Sally Happy Talk' (this newcomer was probably produced under licence); Sally was battery-operated and spoke eight different phrases at the touch of a button. 'Baby Party Doll' was also a hallmark of 1968. Produced under licence from DeLuxe USA, she was able to blow a party squeaker; moving her arms enabled her to blow air.

Some of the other toys produced in 1969 (including those under licence from overseas companies), included: 'Stickle Bricks', 'Glo-Juice', 'Glow-Globs', 'Didgeri Whirler', 'Stack-a-Blocks', the 'Couple Up Game' (from the Lifetime series), the 'Bandit Chase Game', 'Jump Jockey' and 'Spiromatic'.

One important announcement at the end of 1969 was that Pilgrim Pty Ltd (the makers of 'Hi-Speed' wheeled toys), and Cyclops Tri-ang would almost immediately merge. Pilgrim Pty Ltd would however, continue to carry on more or less autonomously as before, with Allen Pilgrim in charge of the Pilgrim operation. Pilgrim Pty Ltd was Australia's second-largest wheeled toy manufacturer at that time, and the biggest manufacturer of golf buggies in Australia.

Over the years Pilgrim had consulted other companies as to the desirability and practicality of merging their technical knowledge with the know-how and industrial experience of Cyclops. They wanted to ensure the stability of the Australian wheeled toy industry. An agreement was negotiated with Cyclops whereby each company would

Cyclops Tri-ang cleaned up at the 1969 Toy of The Year Awards; all the winners were theirs (Courtesy Australasian Sportsgoods and Toy Retailer).

have access to the other's production techniques, personnel skills and space-age technology, but would compete independently for the consumer market as completely autonomous organisations. This type of competition, resulting as it would in increasingly better value products and service, was thought to be of benefit to the whole toy and sporting goods trade as well as to the buying public. At the same time, the merger would be adding to Australia's exports with Pilgrim developing markets for their golf buggies in the USA, Asia, South Africa and New Zealand.

With the completion of the first stage of the new Pilgrim factory (covering 25, 000 sq. ft) on Geelong Road in Brooklyn, Victoria, the increasing demand for the Pilgrim-designed 'Hi-Speed' wheeled toys and golf buggies would be efficiently supplied.

Category	Award	Winner	Manufacturer
Toy of the Year	First Prize	'DeLuxe G.T. Sports Car'	Cyclops Tri-ang
Metal Toys	First Prize	'Wee Waggon'	Cyclops Tri-ang
Wheel Toys	First Prize	'DeLuxe G.T. Sports Car'	Cyclops Tri-ang
Educational	First Prize	Magnetic Play Board	Cyclops Tri-ang

7

1970s Turmoil and Decisions

By the middle of 1970 there were unconfirmed reports from London indicating a crisis in the affairs of the leviathan, Lines Bros. Financial trouble was said to have been in the wind for some time due to over-accelerated expansion and the lack of adequate finance. In fact, this giant toy business had grown into such a world-wide complex that keeping track of it was almost too difficult.

In Australia alone Cyclops Tri-ang, (as the Australian operation was then known), owned its own big operation at Leichhardt in Sydney as well as the Moldex complex in Fairfield, Melbourne. The conglomerate either owned, controlled or had an interest in Pilgrim Pty Ltd of Yarraville (Victoria), Steelcraft of Sunshine (Victoria), the Childcraft Group—which included Tim the Toyman—(Victoria), Affiliated Agencies, Associated Fireworks, Toy Traders and Meccano of Pyrmont in Sydney, A. S. Knight and Hobby & Toy Retailers (Queensland), Joy Toys of Melbourne, H. W. Rice of Sydney and Melbourne, NSW Sports Store, Willis Sports Store (Canberra), and a few others including (much later), Hobbyco of Sydney. The Australian operation had the reputation of being a very profitable one.

Even with all this rumoured upheaval, Cyclops Tri-ang was still introducing new wheeled toys. Among them were a 'G.T. Race Car', cycle bikes (front-wheel driven with American-style semi-pneumatic tyres and outrigger wheels), chain-driven 12" (30 cm) two-wheelers, junior

Above: *The blacksmith's shop where Pilgrim began business in 1946.*
Below: *The Yarraville premises employed over 140 people.*

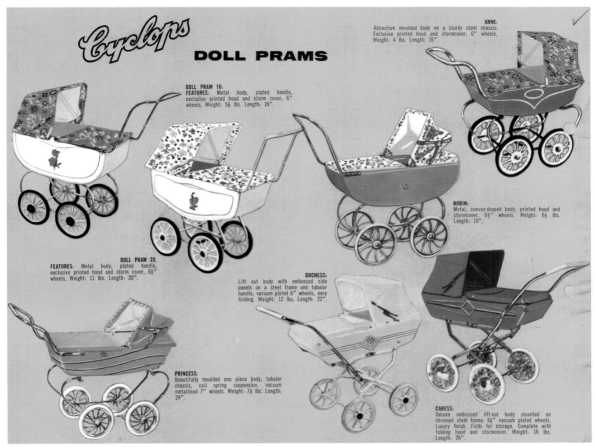

Cyclops
DOLL PRAMS

ANNE:
Attractive moulded body on a sturdy steel chassis. Exclusive printed hood and stormcover. 6" wheels. Weight: 4 lbs. Length: 16".

DOLL PRAM 16:
FEATURES: Metal body, plated handle, exclusive printed hood and storm cover, 6" wheels. Weight: 5½ lbs. Length: 16".

ROBIN:
Metal, convex-shaped body, printed hood and stormcover. 6½" wheels. Weight: 6½ lbs. Length: 19".

DOLL PRAM 20.
FEATURES: Metal body, plated handle, exclusive printed hood and storm cover, 6½" wheels. Weight: 11 lbs. Length: 20".

DUCHESS:
Lift out body with embossed side panels on a steel frame and tubular handle, vacuum plated 6" wheels, easy folding. Weight: 12 lbs. Length: 22".

PRINCESS:
Beautifully moulded one piece body, tubular chassis, coil spring suspension, vacuum metallised 7" wheels. Weight: 7½ lbs. Length: 24".

CARESS:
Deluxe embossed lift-out body mounted on chromed steel frame. 6½" vacuum plated wheels. Luxury finish. Folds for storage. Complete with folding hood and stormcover. Weight: 16 lbs. Length: 26".

From the 1971/72 catalogue—a bright, colouful range of Cyclops dolls' prams

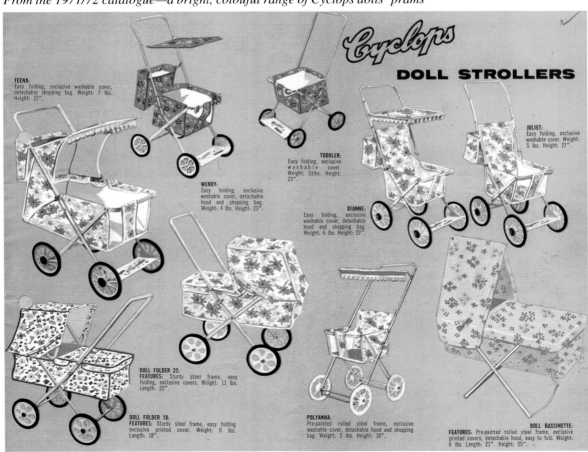

Cyclops
DOLL STROLLERS

TEENA:
Easy folding, exclusive washable cover, detachable shopping bag. Weight: 7 lbs. Height: 27".

JULIET:
Easy folding, exclusive washable cover. Weight: 5 lbs. Height: 27".

TODDLER:
Easy folding, exclusive washable cover. Weight: 3½ lbs. Height: 23".

WENDY:
Easy folding, exclusive washable cover, detachable hood and shopping bag. Weight: 4 lbs. Height: 23".

DIANNE:
Easy folding, exclusive washable cover, detachable hood and shopping bag. Weight: 6 lbs. Height: 27".

DOLL FOLDER 22:
FEATURES: Sturdy steel frame, easy folding, exclusive covers. Weight: 11 lbs. Length: 22".

DOLL FOLDER 18:
FEATURES: Sturdy steel frame, easy folding exclusive printed cover. Weight: 6 lbs. Length: 18".

POLYANNA:
Pre-painted rolled steel frame, exclusive washable cover, detachable hood and shopping bag. Weight: 3 lbs. Height: 30".

DOLL BASSINETTE:
FEATURES: Pre-painted rolled steel frame, exclusive printed covers, detachable hood, easy to fold. Weight: 6 lbs. Length: 21". Height: 25".

Also from the 1971/72 catalogue, floral-covered dolls' strollers

Poster-sized advertisement showing the different Cyclops lines.

The poster included a size chart, a run-down of features, and of course the Cyclops guarantee. Cyclops were the Australian agents for several overseas lines of toys.

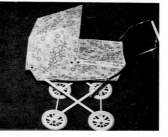

Cyclops present...

THE 'EASY RIDERS' OF 1974

... built to stand the roughest kids, and to handle a whole load of fun!

STANDS 8 and 9 SYDNEY T.A.G.M.A. TOY FAIR from

MARCH 10th to 13th (Inc.)

- Cyclops products helped you reach record sales in '73 . . . see these and new models that will smash records in '74!

CYCLOPS INDUSTRIES PTY. LTD.

(Branches in all States)

A Cyclops TOY IS YOUR Guarantee

Coming attractions; 1974 (From Australasian Sportsgoods and Toy Retailer)   *A boy, his dog and his Cyclops car (Courtesy McWilliams Wines)*

Kings of the track!

...eatures all the ...ofoil, bumper ...s from 48 cm ...99 cm (39")

From the 1976 Cyclops catalogue, another award-winning pedal car

The cover of the 1976 Cyclops catalogue showed a fine variety of their wheeled toys, from the smiling-faced 'Beetle' pedal car to the 'Nursery Walker' at the front of the group.

Product Description	Product Model No.	Packaging	Min. Buy	Trade Price $ each
CARS				
Ferrari	CB07	W/C	1	65.95
Space Cruiser (NEW)	CB08	W/C	1	45.95
Le Mans	CB15	W/C	1	46.95
Off-Road Jeep	CB18	W/C	1	57.95
Army Jeep (NEW)	CB19	W/C	1	57.95
Happy Cart	CB20	W/C	1	46.95
Row Car	CB12	B	1	84.85
TRICYCLES				
Captain Kanga Trike (NEW)	CF80	W/P	6	18.99
* Speedie Dinkie	CF40	W/C	2	22.95
Speedie Dinkie Deluxe	CF41	W/C	2	25.95
Shuttle Trike *NEW COLOUR.*	CF20	W/C	2	31.85
Columbia	CF18	W/C	2	30.95
Police Trike (NEW)	CF60	W/C	2	35.85
Mini Girls (NEW)	CF16	W/C	2	22.95
Mini MX (NEW)	CF65	W/C	2	22.95
Rainbow Trike (NEW)	CF71	W/C	2	25.95
Lil' Miss Trike (NEW)	CF37	W/C	2	32.95
* Dinkie Express	CF45	W/C	2	32.95
Dolly Express	CF55	W/C	2	32.95
Taxi Tipper Deluxe	CF04	W/P	2	37.50
Lawn Dinkie	CF50	W/C	2	36.50
Firebird Trike (NEW)	CF77	W/C	2	39.95
MX Trike (NEW)	CF68	W/C	2	39.95
Mite-Y-Trike (NEW)	CF74	W/C	2	29.95
Senior Tandem	CF26	W/C	1	59.95
PAVEMENT CYCLES				
Cherry	CH20	W/C	1	88.95
Strika	CH15	W/C	1	57.95
Candy	CH28	W/C	1	59.50
Rebel MX	CH36	W/C	1	53.95
Commando (NEW)	CH50	W/C	1	55.95
Sky Pirate (NEW)	CH55	W/C	1	59.95

IMPORTED (Commando, Sky Pirate)

Product Description	Product Model No.	Packaging	Min. Buy	Trade Price $ each
MISCELLANEOUS				
** Convertible Rocker/Table & Bench	CR03	W/C	1	49.95
** Childs Table & Chair Set	CR20	W/P	2	32.50
Victa Mower	CR05	W/C	2	17.95
Dolls Cane Carry Basket	CR08	L	2	10.95
Dolls Plastic Coated Carry Basket	CR10	P	5	5.95
CHARACTER MERCHANDISE				
† Strawberry Shortcake Trike	CK21	W/C	2	32.50
† Strawberry Shortcake Van	CK77	W/C	3	15.99
†† Cabbage Patch Umb. Stroller (New)	CK80	W/C	4	14.95
†† Cabbage Patch Rocker (New)	CK82	W/C	2	15.95
†† Cab. Patch (457mm) Dolls Pram (New)	CK83	W/C	2	26.95
†† Cabbage Patch Sit-n-Ride (New)	CK84	W/C	2	16.75
† Care Bears Bus (New)	CK88	W/C	3	16.75
† Care Bears Trike (New)	CK90	W/C	2	32.50
† Care Bears 30cm Pave. Cycle (New)	CK92	W/C	1	66.95

Product Description	Product Model No.	Packaging	Min. Buy	Trade Price $ each
ROCKERS				
Car Car Rocker	CP03	W/C	2	28.50
Gee Gee Rocker	CP06	W/C	2	28.50
Wooden Rocking Horse (NEW)	CP18	W/C	2	29.95
DOLLS PRAMS AND STROLLERS				
Debbie Cane Pram (NEW)	CL13	W/C	2	29.95
Anne-Marie Cane Pram	CL12	W/C	2	45.95
Walker Pram	CL09	W/C	2	26.95
Susie Moulded Pram (NEW)	CL48	W/C	2	19.75
Victoria	CL25	W/C	1	59.95
Chelsea (NEW)	CL50	W/C	2	29.95
Junior Trio	CL15	W/C	2	43.95
Dianne	CL03	W/C	2	17.95
Super Buggy	CL45	W/C	4	12.95
~~Julie (NEW)~~	~~CL52~~	~~W/C~~	~~2~~	~~25.75~~
LIL' MISS HOMEMAKERS SERIES				
Laundry Trolley	CT03	P	2	13.95
Clothes Hoist	CT04	W/C	3	11.99
Ironing Board *IMPORTED*	CT20	P	5	8.95
Cleaners Set (NEW)	CT35	W/C	1	23.95
SIT-N-RIDES				
Scrambler MX	CS16	W/C	3	16.95
Lil' Girl (NEW)	CS77	W/C	3	16.95
Moon Cruiser	CS24	W/C	3	15.99
Team Cyclops (NEW)	CS83	W/C	3	15.99
Lil' Miss Ride-On (NEW)	CS80	W/C	3	14.99
Tot Tub	CS73	W/C	3	17.50
Beetle Bug	CS68	W/C	3	18.50
BARROWS				
Wheelbarrow 1	CN03	W/C	2	15.99
Wheelbarrow 2	CN06	W/C	2	18.99
Giant Barrow	CN09	W/C	2	26.95
Gardener's Set	CN13	W/C	2	18.75
WAGGONS				
Nursery Walker	CQ10	W/C	2	16.50
Waggon 4	CQ06	W/P	2	23.50
SCOOTERS				
Scooter 6	CJ03	W/C	2	20.95
Scooter 8	CJ06	B	2	38.95

PACKAGING KEY

White Carton with Colour Poster = W/C,

White Carton Printed = W/P

Loose = L, Polythene Bag = P, Brown Carton = B

Price list from 1984, when Cyclops was under the control of T.I. Industries.

GREAT FUN TOYS FOR AUSSIE GIRLS AND BOYS.

Cyclops

Front cover of the 1984 Cyclops catalogue

DOLLY'S DELIGHTS.

Pretty and practical, Cyclops prams, strollers and carry baskets are just like the real thing. They come in a lovely range of styles and colours, and are just the thing for today's modern little miss to really care for that favourite little dolly. 12 month guarantee.

CHELSEA.
Attractive and practical. Folds flat for easy carrying or storage.

JUNIOR TRIO.
The 'everywhichway' pram. Converts from carry basket/bassinette to enclosed pram to fold-up stroller. A dolly's delight.

WALKER PRAM.
A super little pram for the toddling miss. Specially designed for use as a walker.

DEBBIE CANE PRAM.
Pretty little cane bodied pram with lift off hood. Attractively lined.

SUPER BUGGY.
Light and bright. Folds just like an umbrella.

Dolly products from 1984—sadly, most Cyclops products were produced offshore during the 1980s.

THEIR FAVOURITES

Cyclops have searched the globe to find the most lovable toy characters you've ever seen.

Cabbage Patch, Care Bears and Strawberry Shortcake.

These delightful characters have gone straight to the hearts of kiddies all over the world, and they're now available in a superb range of Cyclops designed toys in Australia.

The little brigade will love them.

12 months Guarantee.

CARE BEARS BUS
The original Care Bears Sit-N-Ride. Complete with fun carry bin under seat.
For 1 to 3 year olds.

The wheeled toys bearing well-known children's characters such as 'Care Bears' were an instant success in 1984.

SUPER SIT-ONS.

Each lightweight, yet sturdy unit is a magic adventure for the tiny tot.

Whether it's an all time favourite rocker or a super Sit-N-Ride, most with front wheel steering for co-ordination and balance development, sit them on Cyclops for real fun.

12 months Guarantee.

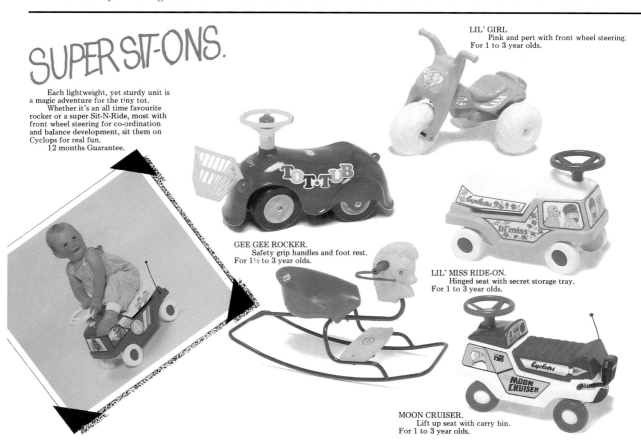

LIL' GIRL
Pink and pert with front wheel steering.
For 1 to 3 year olds.

GEE GEE ROCKER.
Safety grip handles and foot rest.
For 1½ to 3 year olds.

LIL' MISS RIDE-ON.
Hinged seat with secret storage tray.
For 1 to 3 year olds.

MOON CRUISER.
Lift up seat with carry bin.
For 1 to 3 year olds.

Now manufactured in plastic, Cyclops 'Sit'n'Ride' toys are still well-made, well-designed toddlers' playthings.

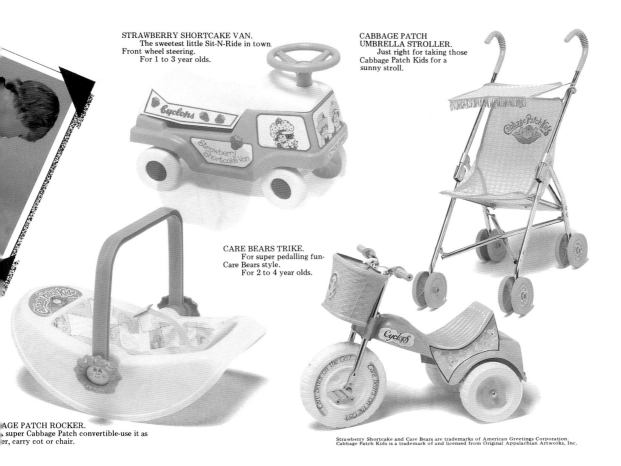

STRAWBERRY SHORTCAKE VAN.
The sweetest little Sit-N-Ride in town.
Front wheel steering.
For 1 to 3 year olds.

**CABBAGE PATCH
UMBRELLA STROLLER.**
Just right for taking those
Cabbage Patch Kids for a
sunny stroll.

CARE BEARS TRIKE.
For super pedalling fun-
Care Bears style.
For 2 to 4 year olds.

...AGE PATCH ROCKER.
...super Cabbage Patch convertible-use it as
...er, carry cot or chair.

Strawberry Shortcake and Care Bears are trademarks of American Greetings Corporation.
Cabbage Patch Kids is a trademark of and licensed from Original Appalachian Artworks, Inc.

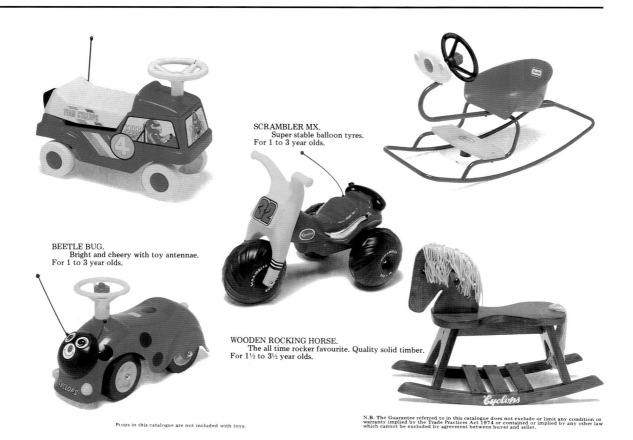

SCRAMBLER MX.
Super stable balloon tyres.
For 1 to 3 year olds.

BEETLE BUG.
Bright and cheery with toy antennae.
For 1 to 3 year olds.

WOODEN ROCKING HORSE.
The all time rocker favourite. Quality solid timber.
For 1½ to 3½ year olds.

Props in this catalogue are not included with toys.

N.B. The Guarantee referred to in this catalogue does not exclude or limit any condition or
warranty implied by the Trade Practices Act 1974 or contained or implied by any other law
which cannot be excluded by agreement between buyer and seller.

The cheerful 'Beetle Bug' was a winner in the 1980s, and the rest of these toys for tots were just as popular

Cyclops toys for boys from the 1980s—another poster-sized advertisement

The best fun toys for Aussie girls and boys.

There's a little bit of magic in a Cyclops toy. The kind of magic that lights up little eyes with the sparkle of excitement, and fills little faces with smiles from ear to ear. The kind of magic that happens only when you're a youngster.

And behind that magic is the quality, reliability and after sales service that has made Cyclops Australia's best loved toy for over 60 years.

Every little child deserves at least one Cyclops toy.

CONVERTIBLE PRAMETTE
As pretty as a picture and as modern as the minute. Converts from seated to reclining positions.

JUNIOR TRIO
The 'everywhichway' pram. Converts from carry basket/bassinette to enclosed pram to fold-up stroller. A dolly's delight.

VICTORIA
Traditionally styled doll's pram finished in quality fabric. Adjustable hood.

WALKER PRAM
A super little pram for the toddling miss. Specially designed for use as a walker.

HAMMOCK STROLLER
A fashionable reclining seat stroller which folds up just like an umbrella.

KOALA STROLLER
Cuddly Koala stroller with furry Koala quilted dolls backrest.

PRINCESS
An elegantly styled doll's pram with stylish chrome steel frame and folding hood.

CAMILLE
A beautiful pram for taking your favourite doll for a stroll. Fold down hood for sunny days.

ANNE-MARIE CANE PRAM
Lovely frilled lining and removable hood.

LAUNDRY TROLLEY
Lift out carry basket.

CABBAGE PATCH UMBRELLA STROLLER
Just right for taking those Cabbage Patch Kids for a sunny stroll.

CHERRY
Stands out in the crowd with stylish moulded lacey wheels. For 4 to 8 year olds.

CABBAGE PATCH PRAM
A superb moulded pram especially designed for your Cabbage Patch doll.

WINKY POP
A super cute, fully equipped girls bike with rear carriers and front basket.

CLOTHES HOIST
A mini version of mums. Complete with rotating hoist.

IRONING BOARD
Helps keep dolly's clothes looking good. One of the 'Lil' Miss Homemaker' series.

Cyclops

BRANCHES AND AGENTS
VICTORIA: T.I. Industries Pty. Ltd., 99 Derby Road, Sunshine, 3020 Tel. (03) 311 0611
NEW SOUTH WALES: T.I. Industries Pty Ltd., 24 William Street, Leichhardt, N.S.W. 2040. Tel. (02) 560 8877
SOUTH AUSTRALIA: T.I. Industries Pty Ltd., 40 Stepney Street, Stepney, 5069. Tel. (08) 42 4591

QUEENSLAND: T.I. Industries Pty Ltd., 246A Evans Road, Salisbury, Queensland, 4107. Tel. (07) 277 8622
TASMANIA: Statewide Importers Pty Ltd., 15 George Street, Launceston, Tasmania, 7250. Tel. (003) 31 2228
WESTERN AUSTRALIA: T.I. Industries Pty Ltd., 82 Robinson Avenue, Belmont, 6104. Tel. (09) 478 2222

Due to our continuing programme of development, Cyclops reserve the right to alter any specification, colour or design without prior notice.
©1986 CABBAGE PATCH KIDS™ is a trademark of and licensed from Original Appalachian Artworks Inc. Cleveland, GA/U.S.A. All Rights Reserved.

On the reverse side, girls' toys from the 1980s

PAVEMENT BIKES

Cyclops REGD.TM
A PART OF GROWING UP IN AUSTRALIA

▲ REAR TO FRONT (L TO R): **CF217** FAIRY GLIDE, **CF2150** BOBCAT, **CF214** LIZARD, **CF213** SHOCKER, **CF2161** STAR GIRL

Range of Cyclops two-wheelers distributed through Hunter's Toyline (1994)

CF225B

CF225P

Cyclops REGD TM
GUARANTEE
FOR LIFE

▲ **CF225B** DINKIE TRIKE

▲ **CF225P** DINKIE TRIKE

Cyclops REGD TM
A PART OF GROWING UP IN AUSTRALIA

New Cyclops Dinkies from Hunter's in 1994, with a reminder of the history behind them.

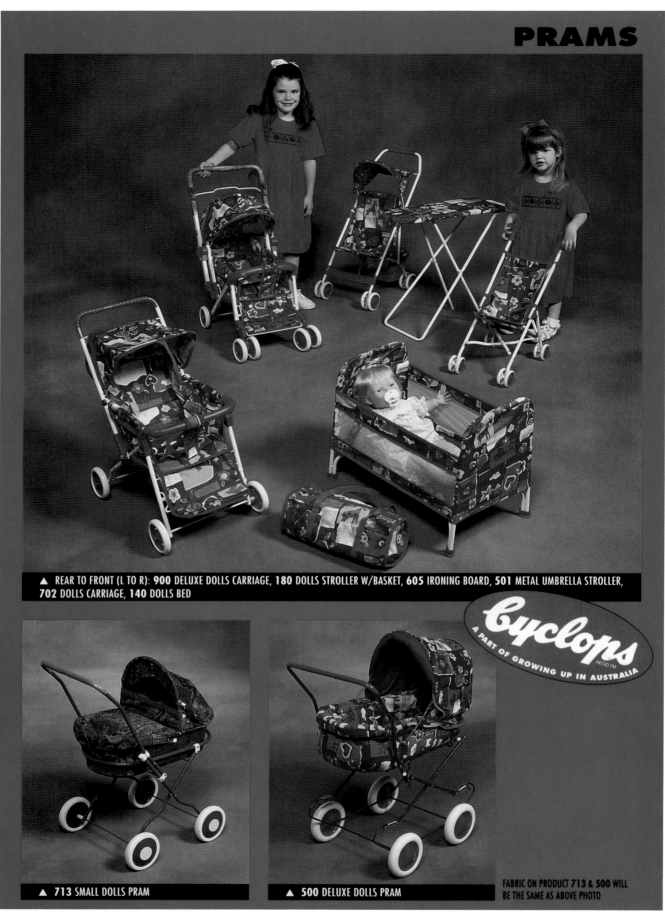

▲ REAR TO FRONT (L TO R): **900** DELUXE DOLLS CARRIAGE, **180** DOLLS STROLLER W/BASKET, **605** IRONING BOARD, **501** METAL UMBRELLA STROLLER, **702** DOLLS CARRIAGE, **140** DOLLS BED

Cyclops
REGD. TM.
A PART OF GROWING UP IN AUSTRALIA

▲ **713** SMALL DOLLS PRAM

▲ **500** DELUXE DOLLS PRAM

FABRIC ON PRODUCT **713** & **500** WILL
BE THE SAME AS ABOVE PHOTO

From Hunter's Toyline catalogue 1994—Australian made Cyclops dolls' products

Wheel Fun

▲ **CF231** JUNIOR TANDEM, **CF230** SENIOR TANDEM, CF223 SCOOTER, **CF229** DOLLY EXPRESS, **CF226** SPEEDIE DINKIE, **CF228** DINKIE EXPRESS

Dinkies and scooters in brightly-coloured plastic (1994), also from the Hunter's catalogue

▲ **CB116** FIRE TRUCK, **CB24** TRACTOR LOADER, **CB111** GOKART

Lifes' greatest adventures begin with

Full circle—Australian made pedal cars, available almost eighty years later

was able to benefit from proven and exciting wheeled toy designs. This was shown in their Cyclops 'Sit'n'Ride' toys; one of these was 'Billy Bird', a big friendly blue bird with a strong moulded body and wide wheels. The appealing bird was only one design from an entire series geared to delight the tots. 'Big Red', with its smoothly moulded body, even had a gear shift and wide track wheel for extra stability. Along with these were 'Percy Pup' and 'Sammy Seal'. All of them were clean, simple designs created by using an entirely new manufacturing process.

Moulded chunky wheels were also a feature of the Cyclops 'Trackka Trike'; this toy's safety features were its extra-wide wheel placement, super-grip front tyre and moulded high-backed seat. The super trike for the 2–4 year olds and 'Taxi Tandem' for 2–5 year olds—a new junior version of the 'Trail Tandem' with an adjustable driving seat, rear seat and super-grip tyres—also sported the new wheels.

Following the sale of the New World domestic appliance business here in Australia and the Tri-ang Pedigree toy business in New Zealand, Tube Investments was to once again review its situation down under.

The theme for the T. A. G. M. A. section of the 1979 Toy Fair was 'Made in Australia', and Cyclops followed this with a selection of their new designs in pedal cars, trikes, scooters and 'Sit'n'Ride' toys. A restyled version of the 'Ferguson Tractor', which had been a big seller in 1978, took pride of place in the display. Also on display was a full range of Cyclops bicycles, including the new BMX version of the 'Amaroo'.

The large building in Leichhardt where Cyclops toys were once made looked a little austere from the outside, but a thriving industry existed within. In the late 1970s an extension was made to the premises in preparation for the establishment of the Raleigh division; this division was to be responsible for the manufacturing and distribution of Raleigh and Cyclops bicycles. The late Sir Hubert Opperman had his picture taken riding a Raleigh cycle in Malta, and he again rode a Raleigh bicycle in 1978—aged 74 years.

From 1 July 1979, the Cyclops and Steelcraft division of T. I. Industries Pty Ltd were to become part of the Raleigh cycle division of T. I. Industries. All their operations were to be reported directly to the Nottingham headquarters.

At the end of 1979 Darcy Reidy, Managing Director of T. I. Industries Pty Ltd (of which Cyclops was a subsidiary), announced that: "We know what our strengths are at Cyclops, and we plan to build on them". Cyclops would certainly be moving more and more into the bicycle field. This was only what was expected, given its connection with Raleigh—the biggest bicycle manufacturer in the world. The plan was to invest substantial sums into updating the equipment at the Leichhardt plant during the next year or so, thus improving the quality of the products while at the same time holding down costs. Innovations in the packaging, graphics and catalogues were proposed for the next year, plus some rationalisation between the Sunshine (Melbourne) and Leichhardt (Sydney) plants.

By August 1979 it had been decided to amalgamate the Australian subsidiaries of Tube Investments Ltd into one company structure—this grouping was to be called T.I. Industries Pty Ltd, and it was to have three operating divisions:

Cyclops (then known as Cyclops Industries Pty Ltd)
New World Appliances (then New World Appliances Pty Ltd)
Steelcraft K & A (then Raleigh Nursery Pty Ltd).

8

1980s Change of Address— Production Goes Offshore

By March 1980 the premier individual brand in Australia was still Cyclops, just like the giant Meccano in the United Kingdom. It was just a reminder of the immense impact that the name of Cyclops had had on the parents and even the grandparents of the 1980s generation of wheeled toy users.

The Cyclops display held at the Sydney Town Hall in 1980 proved this point; it was by far the biggest and best exhibition Cyclops had ever put together. It included a new Cyclops creation—the 'Shuttle Trike'—which won the award for 'Toy of the Year' in a competition for Australian-made toys. The trike also won the Metal Toy Section of the Australian Toy Awards. An Australian design, the 'Shuttle Trike' was made at the Cyclops factory in Leichhardt using a maximum of strong, colourful and fully-moulded components. With a tray at the back that even tipped up to dump whatever load its rider decreed, the toy was aimed at riders aged between three and six years old.

Although many other toy organisations at the display thought that the way of the future was to move with the larger toy groups, Cyclops felt that the small retailer also played an important role in the distribution of their products throughout Australia.

The Raleigh bicycle side of T.I. Industries was developing rapidly in the early eighties, especially the BMX bicycle range. The bike division took part in a very heavy promotional campaign. The sales of BMX bikes had contributed substantially to a wonderful period of trading for both Cyclops and Raleigh; Cyclops enjoyed a record year, with sales recorded at about 15% above budget. Despite the heavy emphasis placed on boys' wheeled toys, Cyclops did not forget their sisters; in the middle of 1980 they launched a new standard 12" (30 cm) cycle named 'Dolly Shopper'. It had a lollipop-pink frame, and came with white accessories and a shopping basket.

The Space Cruiser, with toy helmet and CB radio—from the new look 1984 Cyclops line of pedal cars.

Both sides of the poster-sized 1984 catalogue—four new two-wheelers (bottom right), pre-schoolers' favourites (far right) and the new pedal cars (top right), show the diverse Cyclops range.

In December 1980 the T. I. Industries personnel at Raleigh and Cyclops issued the slogan 'Product Knowledge is Invaluable'. This was particularly pertinent to the changing trend at that time—swinging away from mass merchants and concentrating on the more specialised outlets. One of the reasons for the new slogan was the desire for the smaller retailers to be more conversant with their knowledge of Cyclops products. Due to the projected rise in the birthrate over the next five years a steady demand could be expected, not only of the company's basic lines of prams and pushers (distributed through Steelcraft), but also of their toys for the younger set.

With this thought in mind, Cyclops planned a big revamp of their range at the end of 1980 and proposed a major media campaign in 1981. Following their 1980 successes with the 'Ladybird' and the 'Shuttle Trike', Cyclops would attempt to make the changes to their 1981 toy range the most aggressive for many years in terms of both production and packaging. The media campaign was to be the biggest in the Cyclops company's history.

Cyclops planned to add four new bikes to their 1981 range, having made substantial progress as a bike brand over the last few years. Raleigh cycles also planned to revamp their range in 1981.

In the 1984 catalogue the Cyclops pedal car range had decreased to just seven cars, all with moulded plastic bodies and all designed with the modern up-to-date youngster in mind. They included the new 'Army Jeep', the 'Off Road Jeep', the stylishly designed 'Formula 1 Ferrari', and the European-styled 'Le Mans'. The 'Space Cruiser' with its metallic look, toy CB radio, and super space helmet was also new. Besides the 'Happy Cart' with the lines of a dune buggy, there was the specially designed 'Row Car'; this was hand-operated and therefore also suitable for handicapped children. The eighteen trikes and Dinkies were styled to suit the needs and tastes of a wide range of riders. There were only two scooters included in the range, as this old favourite was fast being superseded by the terrific range of two-wheelers for young children. Both scooters came complete with removable safety outrider trainer wheels.

Young girls were well provided for with nine different styles of prams, one stroller and several carry baskets. When it came to the pre-schoolers, many of the ride-ons carried the names (under licence) of their favourite toys—including 'Strawberry Shortcake', 'Care Bears' and even a 'Cabbage Patch' rocker and stroller.

The old wheelbarrows, still with their rugged steel

frames (one even had a strong pressed metal tray), waggons and motor mowers were still proving popular. These old favourites were little changed; their appearance was more streamlined than the products of the 1940s, but that was all.

The year 1985 was to be the death knell for the old Leichhardt factory, the very basic root of Cyclops operations over the years. Within its walls, children's wheeled toys had evolved from being entirely metal-based to the modern plastic creations of today.

After seventy years as the mainstay of the Cyclops operation, the company shifted its headquarters to Melbourne. This was mainly due to the fact that the T. I. organisation had decided to rationalise their manufacturing division at the Sunshine base where Britax Steelcraft had their head office. Wally Cray moved to Melbourne in early 1985; he was to be the Works Director and he was instrumental in getting the local side of the toy production established on site. When Mr Cray retired in April 1988, his technical expertise and experience were sorely missed.

The 1988 Cyclops (Britax) catalogue contained six pedal cars and one tractor/front-end loader. There were also fifteen bikes, trikes and tandems. Several of these were manufactured in bright pink and aimed at the young female market.

In the dolly vehicle department were four prams, five strollers and even a twin stroller for girls to play with. For the one to three year olds, seven interesting and colourfully designed ride-ons were available, including one named 'Moby' that resembled a whale and the 'Beetle Bug' that looked like a large Ladybird.

In the 'Helping Dad' section there were two wheelbarrows and a waggon, while the 'Little Miss Homemaker' set included an ironing board, a laundry trolley and a clotheshorse.

The sad part about the wonderful range that was available at the end of the 1980s was that the once-proudly Australian name of Cyclops was now being used to promote and distribute a range of toys, the majority of which were being manufactured offshore.

Above: *The old Cyclops Leichhardt factory; awaiting demolition while the toys are manufactured in Melbourne and overseas.*
Below: *The John Heine building that once stood beside the Cyclops factory— already gone.*

Cover of the 1988 Cyclops catalogue (above) and inside pages (below) show how far their range has come since 1913— unfortunately most of the products were not made in Australia

EPILOGUE
THE 1990s—IN AUSTRALIAN HANDS AGAIN

In the early 1990s the famous and much-loved Cyclops name returned to Australian hands. It was bought by Hunter's Toyline, manufacturers of wheeled toys. They are carrying the respected Cyclops name in their large complex at Tullamarine in Melbourne.

So this proud Australian name lives on in the minds and hearts of young and old alike—whether they be men, women, girls or boys. Having survived the Depression years, the war years, the boom, bust and take-over periods of the 1950s through to the 1980s, Cyclops can still capture the style and feel of the current era. Now, hopefully, after over eighty years of giving pleasure to Australian children, the name devised those many long years ago by John Heine will live on to see the beginning of the 21st Century.

The 'Junior Tandem' Ride-on tricycle from the 1995 Hunter's Toyline catalogue.

A COLLECTOR'S GUIDE

CYCLOPS PEDAL CARS—1924–1945

Product	Date	Age Group	Description
No. 0 Motor Car	1924	3–5 years	Crank drive, fitted with patent disc wheels, rubber tyres, headlights and horn. Standard finish in red or blue.
	1932		Model now known as 'Chrysler'
	No date	3–6 yrs	Colours: red, light blue or dark blue; 11" wheels, ½" tyres,.
No. 1 Motor Car	1924	4–8 years	Crank drive, fitted with black enamelled wire wheels. Standard finish red or blue. Rocking pedal drive.
	1932		Crank drive, slightly larger than No. 0, wire wheels and black stove enamelled. Choice of an assortment of body colours in fine lacquer. Complete with horn, headlights and number plate. Specifications: length 37", height 24"; 11" wire wheels, ½" rubber tyres.
No. 22 Motor Car	1924		Body, seasoned pine and sheet steel painted red or blue, lined and varnished. Upholstered in red or blue fabricord. Domed mudguards, nickel-plated mascot. Chain drive, undergear baked black enamel.
No. 24 Motor Car	1924	3–10 years	Chain drive, standard finish—blue, red, grey or brown; upholstered to match. Equipment includes: 5 wire wheels extra-strong, aluminium (Regd.) radiator, bumper, headlights, horn, extra-large steering wheel, windscreen and mascot, wide domed mudguards, aluminium instrument board with embossed clock, speedometer, ammeter and moveable switch.
	1932		Cycle chain drive, finished in two tone lacquer. Fitted with reinforced disc wheels, plated hub caps, heavy balloon tyres, polished aluminium radiator and instrument board, bumpers back and front, windscreen, number plate back and front, headlights, ruby tail light, mascot and horn. Upholstered to tone with body colours. Specifications: length 48", height 26", 11" disc wheels with ¾" fluted rubber tyres.
No. 26 Model	1932		See 'The Sports Model'
No. 28 Model	1932	3–7 years	Chain drive, with reinforced disc wheels. Polished aluminium radiator and dashboard with all modern fittings. Complete with headlights, horn, number plate and mascot. Lacquered in a variety of colours. Specifications: length 38", height 23", 11" disc wheels, ½" rubber tyres.
	1934		Price £5 10s.
No. 30 Motor Car	1932	3–6 years	Cycle chain drive, but otherwise similar to No. 0. Complete with lamps, horn and number plate and metal radiator. Lacquered in a variety of colours. Specifications: length 35", height 23", 11" disc wheels, ½" rubber tyres.
	No date		Colours red or blue, 11" wheels, with ½" tyres.
No. 31 Motor Car	1932		See 'The Straight Eight' Model
	No date	4–8 years	Colours; red, light blue, dark blue, Naples Buff. Wheels—11" with ¾" tyres.

Product	Date	Age Group	Description
Aeroplane		3–7 years	The drive consists of rocking pedals connected to an 11" wheel concealed in the tail. Front wheels are 9" balloon type. Lacquered in striking colour combinations. When the plane is in action the propeller revolves. Specifications: length is 51", height 22"; width across the wings is 21". Back wheel is 11" disc wheel with ½" rubber tyre.
Armoured Car	1940–1	3–7 years	Crank drive; length 43", height 27", all steel construction, designed in imitation of modern war machine. Dummy machine gun swivels horizontally and vertically, has clicking device, which operated by turning a wire handle. Ball bearing back axle. Body stove enamelled in green, mudguards black, cast steering wheel, head lights, number plate, 9" stamped steel spoke wheels, ⅝" rubber tyres—enamelled to match body. Large nickel-plated hub caps. Weight 43 lb. Price: £4 2s 9d ($8.29).
'Bedford' Motor Truck	No date	3–7 years	Colours: combination of red and blue, with 9" wheels and ½" tyres.
	1935		New radiator styling. Colour: combination of red and blue, with 9" wheels and ½" tyres. Weight 35 lb.
	1938		Crank drive, and called 'The Bedford'; length 47", height 21"; all steel chassis, steel tipping tray, 12 x 12" and 4" deep. Hand brake on pressed steel brake drum attached to rear wheel, and ball bearing back axle. Seat and tray stove enamelled red, bonnet and chassis enamelled blue; cast steering wheel, streamlined radiator, horn, headlights, mascot, nickel-plated bumper bar. Stamped steel 9" spoke wheels and ⅝" rubber tyres, enamelled red. Large nickel-plated hub caps. Weight 35 lb.
'Buick'	1935	5–10 years	Colours: red or green. Wheels at 10" and ⅞" tyres. Weight 58 lb.
	1938	5–9 years	Cycle chain drive, length 51" and height 23". Body and chassis of steel, stamped streamlined mudguards. An adjustable seat; chain enclosed in a heavy metal cover. Ball bearing back axle. Body stove enamelled in cream, striped in green, mudguards enamelled green. A hand brake, a streamlined radiator, horn, cast steering wheel, headlights, mascot, number plate, tail light, nickel-plated bumper bars, windscreen, instrument board, moulded rubber step mats. Stamped 10" steel spoke wheels, ⅞" rubber tyres—enamelled green, large nickel-plated hub caps. Weight 58 lb.
	1939		Price £6 12s 6d ($13.25).
'Chevrolet' Model 00D	1932	2–5 years	Crank-driven, this is a similar model to No. 00. There are reinforced balloon disc wheels, lacquered to match body. Metal radiator and number plate. Finished in red or blue lacquer. Specifications: Length 30", height 19", 9" balloon disc wheels with ⅜" rubber tyres.
'Chevrolet' Model 00	1932	2–5 years	Crank drive. Finished in red or blue lacquer. Complete with number plate and metal radiator. Specifications: length 30", height 19" with 9" wire wheels, ⅜" rubber tyres.
'Chevrolet' Car	1939	2–5 years	Crank drive and red enamelled; length 34". Rigid and strong, with 9" spoke wheels and ½" rubber tyres. Price: £2 4s 6d ($4.45).
	1940–41		Crank drive; length 34", height 20", body and chassis of steel, stove enamelled red. Striped in white, cast steering wheel, streamlined radiator and mascot, with 9" brightly tinned wheels, ½" rubber tyres. Weight 23 lb. Price: £1 18s ($3.80).
	1948		Available for a short while, and then radiator changed.
'Chrysler' Model 0	1932	3–6 years	Fitted with reinforced disc wheels, headlights, metal radiator, horn and number plate. Lacquered in a variety of colours. Specifications: length 35", height 23", with 11" disc wheels with ½" rubber tyres.
'Chrysler'	1935	4–8 years	New styling; colours—red or blue. Wheels at 9" and ⅝" tyres. Weight 46 lb.
	1938		Cycle chain drive; length 46", height 22". Body and chassis made of steel. Stamped streamlined mudguards, an adjustable seat, chain enclosed in heavy metal cover, ball bearing back axle. Body stove enamelled red or blue, striped in white, mudguards enamelled to match. Cast steering wheel, streamlined radiator, horn, headlights, mascot, number plate, tail light, nickel-plated bumper bars, a windscreen, and an instrument board. Stamped 9" steel spoke wheels, ⅝" rubber tyres, enamelled to match body, large nickel-plated hub caps.
	1939		Price £5 5s ($10.50).
	1940–41		Body stove enamelled cream, striped in green, mudguards enamelled green, wheels cream. Weight 50½ lb. Price: £2 9s 9d ($5.00).

Product	Date	Age Group	Description
Cyclops Centenary Flyer	No date	3–7 years	Front wheels measure 9" with ⁵⁄₈" tyres. Back wheel measures 7" with ⁵⁄₈" tyres.
	1935		Length 46", height 24", width across wings 27½". Steel framework with sheetmetal body, carved wooden propeller driven by leather belt off front axle, revolving as plane moves along. Front wheels measure 9", ⁵⁄₈" tyres; 7" back wheel, ⁵⁄₈" tyres. Weight 28 lb. Price £2 8s 6d.
Cyclops Motor Truck	1932	3–8 years	Cycle chain drive, exceptionally strong, built on an all steel chassis and riveted so cannot work loose. The tray measures 18" x 18", heaps big enough for passenger or parcels. Reinforced disc wheels. Finished in black and red lacquer. Complete with lamps, horn, radiator cap and number plate. Specifications: length 50" and height overall 25", 11" disc wheels ½" rubber tyres.
	1935	4–8 years	New radiator styling. Colour: red, 10" wheels with ⁷⁄₈" tyres. Weight 47 lb.
	1938		Cycle chain drive; length 54", height 24". Steel tipping tray—15" x 13" and 4" deep, ball bearing back axle. Enamelled red, striped in white, mudguards enamelled to match. Hand brake, cast steering wheel. A streamlined radiator, number plate, horn, headlights, nickel-plated bumper bar and mascot; 10" stamped steel spoke wheels, ⁷⁄₈" rubber tyres, enamelled to match body, large nickel-plated hub caps. Weight 56 lb.
	1939		Length 54", heavier than the Reo; 10" x ⁷⁄₈" wheels, tipping tray, brake and ball bearings. Price: £5 15s ($11.50).
	1940–41		Weight 60 lb. Price: £5 8s ($10.80).
'Dodge'	1935	3–7 years	Colours; red or blue: 9" wheels, ⁵⁄₈" tyres. Weight 33 lb.
	1938		Crank drive; length 42", height 20". Body and chassis constructed entirely out of steel. Ball bearing back axle. Stove enamelled in red or blue and striped in white. Cast steering wheel, streamlined radiator, horn, headlights, mascot, number plate, tail light, nickel-plated bumper bar. Stamped 9" steel spoke wheels with ⁵⁄₈" rubber tyres, enamelled to match body. Large nickel-plated hub caps. Weight 33 lb.
Flivver No. 1	1924	3–6 years	With either wire wheels and steel tyres, or disc wheels and rubber tyres.
	1932		Either with steel tyre wire wheels or reinforced disc wheels, ½" rubber tyres. Framework enamelled black; wheel and seat red.
	1938		Heavy steel frame, steel seat, wooden handle, 11" reinforced disc wheels, ½" rubber tyres. Seat and wheels enamelled red; frame in black.
Flivver No. 2	1924	4–8 years	With either wire wheels and steel tyres, or disc wheels and rubber tyres.
	1932		Similar to No. 1, but much larger.
	1938		Heavy steel frame, steel seat, wooden handle, 11" reinforced disc wheels, ½" rubber tyres, seat and wheels enamelled red; frame in black.
'Hillman' Motor Car	No date	3–7 years	Colours: red, blue or green, 9" wheels ⁵⁄₈" tyres.
Locomotive	1924		Crank drive, steers like a motor car. Painted red, blue or green; lined and varnished. Bright tinned wheels and ½" rubber tyres.
	1924		Rocking pedal drive; could pull a No. 2 Express Waggon as following truck.
	1924		Chain drive.
'Oldsmobile'	1935	4–8 years	Colours red or green; 9" wheels and ⁵⁄₈" tyres. Weight 44 lb.
	1938		Crank drive, length 46" and height 22". The body and chassis entirely of steel; stamped streamlined mudguards, adjustable seat and ball bearing back axle. Stove was enamelled red or green. Striped in white, with the mudguards enamelled to match. A cast steering wheel, streamlined radiator, horn, headlights, mascot and number plate, plus the tail light and the nickel-plated bumper bars. Stamped steel spoke wheels measuring 9" with ⁵⁄₈" rubber tyres, enamelled to match body. Large nickel-plated hub caps. Weight 44 lb.
	1939		Price £4 7s 6d ($8.75).
	1940–41		Body stove enamelled in Yellow Cab yellow, striped in black, mudguards enamelled black. Weight 46 lb. Price: £4 4s 3d ($8.45).

Product	Date	Age Group	Description
'Packard'	1935	5–9 years	Colour red, 10" wheels with $^7/_8$" tyres. Weight 63 lb.
	1938	4–8 years	Cycle chain drive; length 52", height 24", body and chassis of steel. Stamped stream-lined mudguards, chain enclosed in metal cover, roomy folding dickey seat, ball bearing back axle. Body stove enamelled in cream and striped in maroon, mudguards enamelled in maroon. Handbrake, streamlined radiator, horn, cast steering wheel, headlights, mascot, number plate, tail light, nickel-plated bumper bars, windscreen, instrument board, moulded rubber step mats. Stamped 10" steel spoke wheels, $^7/_8$" rubber tyres, enamelled maroon, large nickel-plated hub caps. Weight 63 lb.
	1939		Length 53", height 24". Price: £7 15s ($15.50).
	1940–41		Body stove enamelled cream, striped in red, mudguards red. Electric headlights—fitted with 3½ volt lamps wired to push switch on dash and fitted on chassis to take Eveready Battery 800; wheels cream. Weight 71 lb. Price: £7 10s 9d ($15.10).
'Plymouth'	1935	2–5 years	Colour red, 9" wheels, ½" tyres. Weight 21 lb.
	1938		Crank drive, length 34" and height 20". Body and chassis of steel. Stove enamelled in red, striped in white. Cast steering wheel, streamlined radiator, mascot, 9" brightly tinned wheels, ½" rubber tyres.
'Pontiac'	1935	2–5 years	Colour: red, 9" wheels, $^5/_8$" tyres, weight 27 lb.
	1938		Crank drive, length 34", height 20", body and chassis of steel. Stove enamelled in red, striped in white. Cast steering wheel, streamlined radiator, horn, headlights, mascot. Stamped 9" steel spoke wheels, $^5/_8$" rubber tyres, enamelled to match the body. Large nickel-plated hub caps. Weight 27 lb.
	1939		Price £2 15s ($5.75).
	1940–41		Weight 28 lb.
Pull Waggon (Flivver)	1926		Steel tyred—£1 5s ($2.25), £1 10s ($2.50), rubber tyred £1 15s ($2.75), £2 ($4.00).
Reo Truck	1939	3–7 years	Length 47". All red finish, with truck body, tipping tray, brake and lamps and ball bearings. Price £3 7s 6d ($6.75).
	1940–41		Crank drive; referred to as 'The Reo', length 47", height 21". All steel chassis, steel tipping tray 12" x 12" and 4" deep. Hand brake operates on pressed steel brake drum attached to rear wheel, ball bearing back axle. Stove enamelled red, striped in white. Cast steering wheel, streamlined radiator, horn, headlights, mascot, nickel-plated bumper bar. Stamped 9" steel spoke wheels, $^5/_8$" rubber tyres, enamelled in red. Large nickel-plated hub caps. Weight 37 lb. Price: £3 3s 6d ($6.35).
'Rover' Motor Car	No date	2–5 years	Colours: red, blue or green; 9" wheels and ½" tyres.
'Sports Model' No. 26	1932	3–8 years	Cycle chain drive. Fitted with reinforced disc wheels, heavy balloon tyres, front and back bumpers, hub caps and deep stamped radiator heavily nickel-plated wide domed mudguards. The car came complete with windscreen, headlights, number plate, horn, mascot and instrument board. Finished two tone lacquer in very striking colour combinations. Specifications: length 51", height 26" and 11" disc wheels, ¾" fluted rubber tyres.
Sports V8 Car	1939	3–7 years	Coloured blue, 9" x $^5/_8$" disc wheels, headlamps and horn, nickel-plated bumper bar. Price: £3 7s 6d ($6.75).
	1940–41		Crank drive, length 42" and height 20"; body and chassis of steel. Ball bearing back axle, body stove enamelled in blue, striped in cream, cast steering wheel, stream-lined radiator, horn, headlights, mascot, number plate, tail light and nickel-plated bumper bar. Stamped 9" steel spoke wheels, $^5/_8$" rubber tyres, enamelled in cream. Large nickel-plated hub caps. Weight 33½ lb. Price: £3 0s 6d ($6.50).
'Standard' Motor Car	1930/s	2–5 years	Colours: red, blue or green; 9" wheels and ½" tyres.
'Star' Motor Car	1930	3–5 years	Length 30", red enamelled, strongly constructed, rubber tyres. Price: £2 2s 6d ($4.60).
	1932	2–5 years	Crank drive, metal radiator and number plate. Finished in red or blue lacquer. Specifications: length 30", height 19". Wheels 9", $^3/_8$" rubber tyres.
'Star D' Motor Car	1932	2–5 years	Crank drive, it is the 'Star Car' but with disc instead of wire wheels. Metal radiator and number plate. Specifications: length at 30" and height at 19"; 9" disc wheels, with $^3/_8$" rubber tyres.

Product	Date	Age Group	Description
'Straight Eight' Model No. 31	1930	3–8 years	Cycle chain drive; length 44", with 11" balloon disc wheels. Lacquer finish, plated radiator, efficient brake, horn, headlight and windscreen. Price: £7 5s ($14.25).
	1932		Cycle chain drive, lacquer finish, with attractive stripes in contrasting colours. Full balloon disc wheels, hub caps and deep stamped radiator heavily nickel-plated. Extra-wide domed mudguards, running boards trimmed with aluminium edging. An efficient brake that operates on pressed steel brake drums. Complete with horn, headlights, windscreen, mascot, number plate and instrument board. Specifications: length 44", height 24", 11" balloon disc wheels, ¾" rubber tyres.
'The Vauxhall'	1940–41	4–8 years	Cycle chain drive; length 44½", height 21". Body and chassis of steel, adjustable seat, chain enclosed in heavy metal cover. Ball bearing back axle. Stove enamelled red, striped in cream, cast steering wheel, streamlined radiator, horn, headlights, mascot, number plate, tail light and a nickel-plated bumper bar. Stamped 9" steel spoke wheels, ⁵/₈" rubber tyres, enamelled in cream. Large nickel-plated hub caps. Weight 39 lb. Price: £4 3s 6d ($8.35).

DOLLS' PRAMS

Product	Date	Age Group	Description
Cyclops Doll's Pram	1939		English style, constructed of steel, lacquered in colour combinations of sky blue, fawn or pink with cream panel. Collapsible cloth hood and rubber tyred cushion wheels. Length of body 19". Price: £1 15s ($3.50).
Doll's Pram No. 1	1932		Steel body, lacquered in striking colour combinations. Specifications: body length overall 19", width 9¼" depth 9¼", wire wheels 5" diameter, with ³/₈" rubber tyres.
	1938		Light steel panels, 19" overall, width 9¼", depth 9¼". Strong material collapsible hood covered in colours to match body. Wheels measured 6", ½" ribbed tyres, stove enamelled cream, nickel-plated hub caps. Undergear and handles enamelled cream, body lacquered in following combinations: sky blue with cream panel, fawn with cream panel or pink with cream panel. Weight 9 lb. Price: £1 8s 6d ($2.85).
Doll's Pram No. 2	1932		Larger than 'Doll's Pram No. 1', with tubular handlebar, steel body, lacquered in two-tone combinations. Length overall 21", the width 10" and depth 10"; 7" wire wheels, ½" rubber tyres.
	1938		Light steel panels, lined with fibre board. Length 21" overall, 10" wide and 10" deep. Strong material collapsible hood, in colours to match body. Wheels 7", ½" ribbed tyres, stove enamelled in cream, nickel-plated hub caps. The undergear and handles enamelled cream, body lacquered either sky blue with cream panel, fawn with cream panel, pink with cream panel. Weight 13 lb. Price: £1 17s 3d ($3.70).
Doll's Strollette	1938		Made of best quality pine, fitted with folding arm rests and body strap. Back wheels 7", ½" rubber tyres. Front wheels 6", ³/₈" rubber tyres and nickel-plated hub caps. Enamelled in blue, green or orange, striped deckchair canvas to tone. Obtainable with or without hood. Weight without hood 7 lb; with hood 8 lb.
	1939		Folding pattern, wooden frame, rubber tyred wheels, striped canvas: with hood £1 1s 6d ($2.15), without hood 18s ($1.80).

CYCLOPS PEDAL CARS—POST-1950

Army Patrol Car—(3–7 years)

1968   Crank drive; length 39", width 17½". Weight 32 lb, 7½"
              pressed metal spoke wheels, heavy duty tyres. Body of
              pressed metal with strong box section, section sides,
              adjustable rubber pedals. Has helmet, removable jerry
              can, aerial flag. Glossy green body, with white wheels,
              army markings and trim. Price: $30.95

Army Rocket Jeep—(3–7 yrs)

1961–62   Crank drive; length 36", width 17½". Weight 33 lb, 8½"
              artillery type wheels, ⅝" tyres with chrome-plated hub
              caps. A delight for young 'Rocketeers'. Steel body,
              safety rolled edges, adjustable pedals, ball bearing rear
              axle. Realistic jeep radiator grille, headlights and bumper
              bar. Imitation rocket with safety rubber nose cone. U.S.
              army markings. Jungle green, white wheels. New in
              1961, (see under **Jeep** for other Jeep cars).

Army Staff Car—(Not in 1968 catalogue)

1967   Crank drive (adjustable); length 35", width 15".
              Weight 19 lb, 7½" 'laced' pressed steel wheels
              moulded rubber tyres. Steel body with special
              features—dummy field telephone and helmet.
              Finished army green with army markings.

'Bantam'—(Suit child 18 months–3 yrs)

1960   Crank drive; length 25", width 15½". Weight 10 lb, 6"
              diameter wheels with ½" rubber tyres. Steel body with
              safety rolled edges, adjustable pedals. Could be used as
              a pushalong toy. Red body, white wheels. New in 1960.
1961–62   End of production. Side panels altered, pressed
              metal artillery type wheels, and car painted blue with
              white wheels.

'Bermuda'—(3–7 yrs)

1968   Length 39"; weight 28 lb, 7½" pressed spoke
              wheels. Ultra-modern pressed steel body with adjustable
              back rest and pedals. Chrome wire windscreen. Red
              enamelled body, white wheels and trim. Price: $28.95

'Car Thirty'—(2–5 yrs)

1956   Crank drive; length 35", width 14". Weight 20 lb, 7" disc
              wheels. ½" rubber tyres, nickel-plated hub caps,
              streamlined styling, adjustable pedals. Body enamelled
              golden yellow with black lining and decor. Steering
              wheel and windshield black. Radiator, headlights and
              wheels ivory. Last produced in 1957 (see under **Thirty**).
1957   Wheels 7", finished in white.

'Chevrolet'—(2–5 yrs)

1950–51   Soundly constructed with spoke wheels. Price £2 2s 6d.
1951–52   Price £2 13s 6d ($5.35).

'Clipper'—(3–7 yrs)

1953   Adjustable seat, ball bearing back axle, 47" long,
     20" high and 16" wide. Price: £16 7s 6d ($32.75).

1954–55 Crank drive with ball bearings fitted to back axle; length
     46", width 17¼" and 20" high. Weight 42 lb, body
     constructed of steel, streamlined. Adjustable seat, nickel-
     plated radiator grille and headlights, number plate, tail
     light, nickel-plated bumper bars (rear and front) and horn.
     Balloon disc 9" wheels, with ⅝" rubber tyres, large
     nickel-plated hub caps, enamelled red and lined cream.
     Suit child aged 3–8 years, (see under **Ford Clipper**).

1956–57 Radiator grille enamelled ivory. Enamelled red,
     lined ivory. Red and white wheels to give white wall
     effect.

'Comet'—(2–5 yrs)

1953   Length 34", height 20". Price: £8 5s ($16.50).

1954–55 Crank drive; length 34", width 17¼". Weight 24½ lb;
     steel body, streamlined radiator, mascot. 8½" disc wheels,
     ⅝" rubber tyres, large nickel-plated hub caps. Body
     enamelled blue, lined white, wheels white.
     Price (in 1955): £8 10s 6d ($17.05).

1956–59 Adjustable pedals; 17¾" wide. Weight 24½ lb

1960–61 Artillery type wheels 8½" with ⅝" rubber tyres.
     Weight 25 lb. 'Blisters' on sides. Car blue with white
     wheels.

1963–65 Same as 1960–61 version, but car now has flatter
     nose, pressed metal multi-spoke wheels. Finished
     blue, white wheels.

1967   Same as 1963–65 model, but has artillery type wheels,
     same as 1960–61 version. New transfer on side, no
     racing number.

1968–69 White pressed steel 'lace' multi-spoked wheels, winged
     transfer on front. Last produced in 1969. Price: $22.95.

Crash Waggon—(3–7 yrs)

1954–55 Crank drive with ball bearing axle; length 51",
     width 17½". Weight 36½ lb; welded, heavy gauge steel
     body. Crane—sturdy pressed steel with ratchet controlled
     hoisting gear. Lifts and tows another pedal car. Modern
     radiator grille, headlights and radiator cap. Nickel-plated
     front bumper bar mounted on rubber buffers; also comes
     with horn. Disc wheels at 8½" with ⅝" rubber tyres.
     Large nickel-plated hub caps. Body enamelled red, crane
     green; wheels white. Price: £11 5s ($22.95).

1956   Adjustable pedals.

'Dart'—(2–4 yrs)

1956–57 Crank drive; length 29", width 16". Weight 14 lb, 7" disc
     wheels, ½" rubber tyres, nickel-plated hub caps. Body of
     steel with safety edges. Pressed metal curved radiator.
     Body enamelled red, wheels and steering wheel
     enamelled white, (see under 'Prince' for deluxe version).

1959–63 White stencil on side.

1964   As previous model, but now has 7" pressed steel
     multi-spoke wheels.

1967   Yellow painted ribbed disc wheels, has lining on
     bonnet.

1968–69 White ribbed disc wheels. Price: $19.50.

'Dart Express'—Locomotive—(2–4 yrs)

1967   Crank drive; length 29", width 16". Weight 15 lb; 7" disc
            wheels, chromed hub caps. Features locomotive cab front,
            smoke stack, cow catcher and other details. Body finished
            red, with yellow wheels.

Dragster Racer—(4–8 years)

1965   Crank drive; length 39", width 21". Weight 26 lb; 8½"
            artillery type wheels with super cushion tyres. Sturdy
            tubular steel frame, adjustable pedals, ball bearing rear
            axle. Back rest, built in footplate at rear for the pedal car
            'pusher' or 'passenger'. Extra width for stability.
            Brilliant red finish, white wheels.

Fire Chief Waggon—(3–7 yrs)

1967   Crank drive; length 44", width 17½". Artillery wheels
            at 8½", with plated hub caps. Features adjustable
            rubber pedals, realistic Jeep grille and bumper bar.
            Special features include dummy headlights, detachable
            ladder, Fire Chief's helmet, radio aerial, dummy
            telephone, real sound siren, hose attached to revolving
            hose drum and fire engine markings. Body red enamel,
            wheels white; (see under **Jeep**).

Fire Engine—(2–6 yrs)

1968   Crank drive; length 38", width 15". Weight 21 lb; 7½"
            pressed metal 'laced' wheels and chrome-plated hub
            caps. Pressed metal body, adjustable pedals, bell,
            plastic hose mounted on revolving drum, complete
            with nozzle and tap fittings. Finished in brilliant fire
            engine red, with appropriate transfers and markings.
            Price: $28.95.

1969–70/71 Model same as 1968, but without hose reel and
            hose.

1971/72   Length 35"; 6½" 'laced' wheels. Weight 20 lb, looks the
            same as 1970/71 version. Suit child aged 2–5 years.

Fire Engine Jeep—(3–7 yrs)

1959–60   Crank drive; length 36", width 17½". Weight 33 lb, 8½"
            pressed steel artillery type wheels, ⁵⁄₈" tyres, chrome hub
            caps. Steel body, rolled edges, adjustable pedals, ball
            bearing back axle. Jeep grille, headlights and bumper bar.
            Folding windscreen. Two detachable wooden ladders, fire
            bell that rings, and a plastic fireman's helmet. Finish:
            fire engine red, bright yellow wheels, windshield and trim.

1961   Same vehicle as 1959–60 but has white wheels and wind-
            shield, with yellow trim.

1963   Same as 1961, but a dummy fire extinguisher was added.

Fire Waggon—(3–7 yrs)

1962–65   Crank drive; length 51", width 17½". Weight 36 lb; 8½"
            artillery type wheels, ⁵⁄₈" rubber tyres. Welded steel
            body, adjustable pedals, ball bearing to back axle,
            chrome-plated front bumper bar and hub caps. Rear
            'crew' department, with chrome-plated tubular hand
            rails. Fire bell that rings and a fireman's plastic helmet.
            Detachable wooden ladder, body finished in brilliant red,
            with wheels, windshield and steering wheel in white.

'Ford Clipper'—(3–6 yrs)

1950   Streamlined pedal car; (see under **Clipper**)
            Price: £10 5s ($20.50).

1951–52   Price: £13 7s 9d ($26.79).

General's Jeep—(3–7 yrs)

1967   Super model of the Pentropic Jeep. Special features:
            dummy field telephone, jerry can, spare wheel radio
            aerial, tin helmet, General's pennant and command
            markings.

Go-Kart—(4–8 yrs)

1960   Combination crank and chain drive with 2 to 1 upwards ratio, (ensures fast getaway with smoothness and safety); length 47". Weight 29 lb; 10" pressed steel artillery type wheels. The first Go-Kart for younger children, heavy duty all welded tubular steel frame, adjustable pedals, upholstered seat and back rest, safety brake.

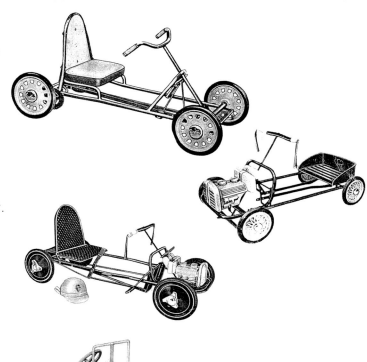

Go-Kart Junior—(4–8 yrs)

1961–63   Crank drive; length 33", width 21". Weight 20 lb; sparkling chrome 'lace' wheels, heavy duty moulded tyres. Sturdy tubular steel frame, adjustable pedals, upholstered seat. Wide wheel track for safety. Finish: stove enamelled gleaming red with white plastic 'skid-lid'.

Go-Kart Senior—(6–10 yrs)

1961–63   Crank drive; length 43", width 22". Weight 31 lb; 9" diameter wheels, with balloon tyres. Heavy duty all welded tube steel frame, crank drive, ball bearing to back axle, adjustable pedals, upholstered seat and back rest, safety brake. Built in footplate at rear for 'pusher' or 'passenger'. Plastic 'skid-lid', Finished in red enamel with red and white disc wheels.

Jeep—(3–7 yrs)

1955–57   Crank drive; length 36", width 17½". Weight 30 lb; body constructed of heavy gauge steel, with ball bearings to back axle. Realistic Jeep radiator grille, headlights and bumper bar. Folding windscreen, 8½" disc wheels with ⅝" rubber tyres. Large nickel-plated hub caps. Body enamelled dark green with appropriate (U.S.) army markings.

1959   Same model as 1955–57, but has 8½" artillery pressed steel wheels, ⅝" tyres with chrome-plated hub caps and adjustable pedals. Spare wheel and number plate have been added. Body enamelled 'jungle green' with U.S. army markings.

Jeep Scout Car

1960   Same dimensions as Jeep of 1957–59; 8½" artillery wheels, ⅝" tyres and chrome-plated hub caps. Steel body, safety rolled edges. Number plate and distinctive pennant. Body enamelled yellow and wheels white.

'Jupiter'—(3–7 yrs)

1956   Crank drive; length 40", width 20". Weight 36 lb; 8½" disc wheels, with ⅝" rubber tyres and large nickel-plated hub caps. Welded heavy gauge pressed steel, modern styling, with ball bearings on rear axle, adjustable pedals, nickel-plated head lamps, windshield, horn and number plate. Body finished in high gloss enamel. Radiator, windshield, steering wheel and wheels, ivory.

1957   Dimensions as per 1956 model, with 8½" artillery wheels enamelled white with plated hub caps. Number plate, windshield and dummy gear lever (with three positions). Body enamelled brilliant 'two-tone' blue, with gloss white trimmings, name, steering wheel and windshield.

1959   Same as previous Jupiter, but had chrome-plated headlights and radiator grille. Body enamelled brilliant 'two-tone' with gloss white trim.

1960   Same as previous Jupiter, but with opening bonnet.

'Lightning'—(3–7 yrs)

1959   Crank drive; length 37", height 17½" and width 17½". Weight 36 lb; 8½" disc wheels with rubber tyres and plated hub caps. Body of welded sheet steel with exceptionally strong box section sides with safety edges. Rubber pedals, adjustable for length. Chrome-plated front bumper bar, headlights, parking lights, radiator grille and windshield. Rear panel had twin tail lights and number plate. Body enamelled gloss yellow with white wheels, black steering wheel and trim.

1960   Wheels; artillery type with rubber tyres and plated hub caps. Body enamelled brilliant red, with steering wheel, wheels and trimmings in white.

1961   Same as 1960 model, but with new logo and stencils on sides.

1963–65   As per 1961 model, but now has large capacity boot with opening door, heavy duty rubber tyres and chrome-plated hub caps.

1967   Dimensions as before. Streamlined carry bin at rear. 'Blisters' removed from front hood panel. Chrome-plated bumper bar, dummy headlights, grill, parking lights and windshield. Body finished red with streamlined logo along sides.

1968   Length 39" and width 17½". Weight 32 lb; 7½" artillery wheels and heavy duty tyres. Body has strong box section sides, crank drive, adjustable rubber pedals and oval steering wheel. Chrome-plated realistic bumper bar, dummy headlights, grille, park lights, and windshield. Carry bin has been removed from body. Body finished in brilliant poly-chromatic enamel. Price: $28.95.

1970/71   As previous model, but with new racing decor.

1971/72   As previous model, but has pressed metal body.

'Morris Oxford'—(3–7 yrs)

1963–64   Length 43" and width 17½". Weight 30 lb; chrome-plated pressed metal wheels with cushion tyres. Welded steel body with safety rolled edges. Combined pedal and seat back, adjustable to a leg length of 20"–25". Fitted with opening bonnet and boot, plus electrically operated lights and horn (using Eveready batteries No. 950). Chromed radiator grille of authentic design, white plastic bumpers and headlight shield. Stove enamelled brilliant two-tone body.

Pentropic Jeep—(3–7 yrs)

1963–65   Dimensions and wheels same as Jeep of 1959. Realistic Jeep radiator grille, headlights and bumper bar. Fitted with jerry can, dummy field telephone and spare wheel. Army markings. Body painted jungle green, with white wheels.

1967   Length 35", with jerry can, tin helmet and army markings.

Police Car—(3–7 yrs)

1960–62   Crank drive; length 36", width 17½". Weight 31 lb; 8½" artillery wheels, ⅝" rubber tyres and chrome-plated hub caps. Welded steel body, safety edges, crank drive, adjustable pedals, ball bearings on rear axle, modern radiator grille with welded headlights and windshield, chrome-plated bumper bar. 'Flying Squad' decoration on door panels. Fitted with bell that rings, radio aerial and revolver in built in holster. Body enamelled blue, and wheels white; (see under **Squad Car**).

Police Car—(2–6 yrs)

1965   New design; length 35", width 15". Weight 19 lb; 7½" pressed metal 'laced' wheels, moulded cushion tyres. Modern styling, adjustable pedals, windshield and horn. Body enamelled deep blue with 'Squad Car' emblems. Grille and wheels white.

1967–68   Different front grille to 1965 model—ringing bell replaces siren; larger 'Squad Car' emblem on sides. Price: $24.95.

'Prince'—(2–4 yrs)

1957   Weight 15½ lb. DeLuxe version of Dart Car. Model features pressed metal windshield, horn and nickel-plated radiator grille and mascot. Enamelled blue with yellow wheels and white steering wheel; (see under **Dart** car).

1959   As previous model, but has chrome-plated radiator grille, windshield and mascot.

Radio Taxi—(3–7 yrs)

1957   Crank drive; length 42", width 17½". Weight 31 lb; 8½" artillery type wheels and plated hub caps. Welded steel body, adjustable pedals with ball bearing to rear axle. Chrome radiator grille, headlights, mascot and bumper bar mounted on rubber buffers. Fittings included windshield, dummy gearshift, horn and flexible radio aerial. Car finished in brilliant red and white enamel with blue wheels.

1959–60   Similar to 1957 model, but with different gleaming chrome bumper bar. It also had tail lights.

'Rambler'—(2–6 yrs)

1960–61   Length 35" and width 15". Weight 19½ lb; 7½" chrome-plated pressed metal wheels with white cushion tyres. Ultra-modern styling, featuring electric lights, and an electric horn (Eveready 950 torch batteries were used), with built in battery box. Chrome-plated swept back windshield, front and rear grilles with integral bumper bars, adjustable pedals, and number plates (front and rear). Stove enamelled in brilliant two-tone blue and white.

1963   As 1960 model, but has opening boot and bonnet, with realistic dummy engine.

'Sixty'—(3–7 yrs)

1954–55   Crank drive; length 42", width 17½". Weight 30½ lb; body of welded, heavy gauge pressed steel, with ball bearings fitted to back axle. Modern radiator grille, headlights and radiator cap. Nickel-plated front bumper bar mounted on rubber buffers. Number plate, 8½" disc wheels, ⅝" rubber tyres and large nickel-plated hub caps. Body enamelled blue and the wheels white; (see under **Sixty Tip**).

1955   Horn added.

1956   Adjustable pedals.

'Sixty Tip'—(3–7 yrs)

1957   Crank drive; length 47½", width 17½". Weight 32 lb; 8½" disc wheels, ⅝" tyres and nickel-plated hub caps. Welded steel body, safety edges, lever operated, large capacity tipper bin. Adjustable pedals, ball races to rear axle. Plated bumper bar mounted on rubber buffers, horn and windshield. Body enamelled blue with red tray, white wheels, windshield and steering wheel. 'Cyclops Contractors' emblem on door panel.

1959–61   Model as before, but with latest style radiator grille with cowled headlights, chrome-plated hub caps and new style bumper bar.

Skat Kar—(4–8 yrs)

1961   Crank drive; length 37½", width 22½". Weight 25 lb;
              front wheels 7" diameter and rear wheels were 8½"
              disc type. Model was a replica of the famous American
              'drag strip' racers of the time. Features included tubular
              steel frame, crank drive, adjustable pedals and safety
              back rest on seat. Stove enamelled red, with white
              wheels; (see under **Go-Karts**).

Skat Kart—(2–4 yrs)

1970–72   Wide wheels, strong tubular metal frame, moulded
              plastic safety bucket seat, plastic helmet. Weight 7 lb;
              length 26½". 'At last! Here's a 'Riding' toy for youngsters
              barely able to walk'. Safe even for the very young, it has a
              sports car flair and allows even the smallest tot to 'reach
              the pedals'; (only the frame of this cart was metal).
1976   Weight 6.8 lb; length 24".

Squad Car—(2–5 yrs)

1970/71   Crank drive; length 35", width 15". Weight 19 lb; 7½"
              'laced' pressed steel metal wheels, moulded cushion tyres,
              chromed hub caps. Pressed metal body, adjustable pedals,
              windshield, bell, police emblems, including large 'Squad
              Car' emblem along side panels. Deep blue enamelled
              body; wheels and grille white; (see under **Police Car**).
1971/72   Wheels now 6½" 'laced' wheels.

Station Waggon—(3–7 yrs)

1954   Crank drive; length 51", 17½" wide. Weight 35 lb; welded
              heavy gauge pressed steel body with large rear goods
              compartment and opening tailboard, ball bearings to back
              axle. Modern radiator grille, headlights and radiator cap.
              Nickel-plated handrails. Nickel-plated front bumper bar
              mounted on rubber buffers. Number plate, 8½" disc
              wheels, ⁵⁄₈" rubber tyres. Large nickel-plated hub caps.
              Body enamelled red, wheels white.
1955   Horn added.
1956   Adjustable pedals.
1957   Artillery wheels at 8½"; plated hub caps, body enamelled red
              in red, wheels yellow, with white windscreen and steering
              wheel.
1959–61   Latest style radiator grille, headlights and radiator cap,
              chrome-plated hand rail, and new style chrome-plated
              bumper bar. Number plate.

Super Scooper—(2–5 yrs)

1959–60   Length 44" and width 17¾". Weight 31 lb; based on
              the sturdy Comet car, the Super Scooper featured a
              roomy front loading scoop. This is operated from the
              driver's seat by separate lever controls for elevating
              and dumping. Body enamelled red, the scoop in blue
              and the wheels in white.

'Thirty'—(2–5 yrs)

1956   Crank drive; length 35", width 14". Weight 20 lb; 7" disc
              wheels, ½" rubber tyres, nickel-plated hub caps. Body of
              welded heavy gauge pressed steel with streamlined
              styling, adjustable pedals. Body enamelled golden
              yellow with black lining and decor. Steering wheel and
              windshield black. Radiator, headlights and wheels done
              in ivory; (see under **Car Thirty**).
1957   Wheels measured 7"; finished in white.

'Thunderbird'—(2–6 yrs)

1962–65   Pressed 7½" metal multi-spoke wheels, with moulded cushion tyres. Ultra-modern styling, same as Rambler car; enamelled front and rear grilles. Adjustable pedals, swept back windshield. Stove enamelled red, grille and wheels white.

1967   Similar to 1962–65 model with large Thunderbird logo on side panels. Chrome-plated hub caps.

1968   As before; blue with 'laced' spoke\d wheels, padded seat and oval steering wheel. Brilliant poly-chromatic enamel, wheels white, chromed grille. Price: $25.95.

'Thunderbird with Bin'—(2–5 yrs)

1970/71   Crank drive; length 41", width 15". Weight 19 lb; wheels 6½" 'laced' pressed metal wheels with cushion tyres. Pressed metal body, adjustable pedals, windshield, padded seat, lever operated tip bin in contrasting colour. Body finished in brilliant poly-chromatic enamel, wheels white.

1971/72   Same as 1970/71 version, but with upholstered seat.

Tip Truck—(2–5 yrs)

1954–55   Crank drive; length 45", width 17¾". Weight 28 lb; 8½" disc wheels with ⅝" rubber tyres, large nickel-plated hub caps. Body constructed of steel with a tipping tray 12" x 12" and 4" deep, streamlined radiator and mascot. Body enamelled red, lined white, with white wheels.

1956   Adjustable pedals.

1957   Similar to 1956 model, but body enamelled in red, tray blue, and wheels white.

1959   Now with chrome-plated hub caps and mascot.

1960   A clip-on loading shovel added; total weight 29 lb.

1961   Same as 1960 model, but wheels changed to artillery type.

1963–65   A new flat front on radiator, replacing the curved radiator. Thin pressed metal spokes on artillery wheels.

1967   Wide 8½" spoke artillery wheels. Words 'Sand, Gravel, Metal' on side panels.

1968   Fine 7½" spoke artillery wheels. New logo on side and a transfer on top of the radiator. Price: $26.95.

'Traveller'—(3–7 yrs)

1968   Length 39" and 7½" white artillery wheels. Weight 29 lb; pressed metal body, adjustable back rest and pedals. Gleaming chrome grilles back and front, chrome wire windscreen, oval steering wheel. Brilliant poly-chromatic enamel finish with white trim, including long 'Traveller' logo on side panels. Price: $30.95.

1970/71   Not included in catalogue.

1971/72   Same as 1968 car.

'Triumph Herald'—(18 mons–3 yrs)

1963   Crank drive; length 28", width 14". Weight 15 lb; 6" diameter artillery wheels, moulded rubber tyres. Pressed metal body, adjustable pedals. Body enamelled red, wheels white.

1964   Not in catalogue.

1965   Same as 1963 model.

Veteran Car—(3–7 yrs)

1963–64   Crank drive (adjustable); length 36", width 21" Weight 26 lb; Spoked wheels, 10" front, 12" rear wheels, sprung back axle. An old world touch. Pressed metal body, fitted with individual mudguards, 2 front lamps, rubber bulb horn, starting handle with ratchet noise. Brilliantly enamelled in green and yellow.

Zephr—(3–7 yrs)

1960–62   Crank drive; length 40", width 20". Weight 38 lb; 8½"
           artillery wheels. Welded pressed steel body, adjustable
           rubber pedals, ball bearings on back axle. Chrome-plated
           radiator grille, windshield and hub caps. Opening bonnet
           for access to realistic dummy engine. Battery operated electric
           lights. Finished in glossy two tone, with white wheels
           and trim.

TRACTORS AND OTHER CRANK-DRIVE VEHICLES POST-1950

Cyclops Major Tractor—(3–7 yrs)

1957   Crank drive; length 36", height 27" and width 20". Main
           body member of 1¼" diameter solid drawn tubular steel.
           Large, comfortable pressed metal tractor seat. Rubber
           exhaust pipe, tractor type radiator and mudguards on the
           rear wheels. Provision for tow bar on main member.
           Adjustable pedals. Balloon 9" disc wheels with ⅝"
           rubber tyres and large nickel-plated hub caps on rear
           wheels. Enamelled red finish with illustration of engine
           on bonnet sides. Seat white.
1960–61   Dummy gear shift lever.
1963   Enamelled blue, yellow wheels.

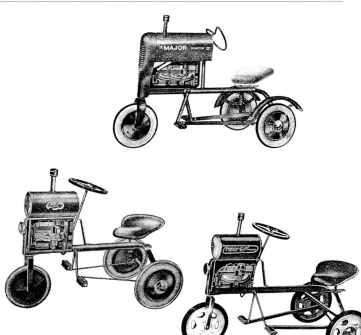

Cyclops Minor Tractor—(3–6 yrs)

1956–57   Crank drive; length 32", height 25" and width 16". Weight
           18 lb; main member of
           body 1¼" diameter solid drawn tubular steel.
           Large, comfortable pressed metal adjustable tractor seat.
           Rubber exhaust pipe. Nickel-plated head-
           light. Provision for tow bar on main member. Disc
           front wheel at 8", ¾" rubber tyre. Balloon disc rear
           wheels 9", ⅝" rubber tyres and large nickel-plated hub
           caps. Enamelled golden yellow with illustration of
           engine on bonnet sides. Price: £7 15s ($15.50).
1959   Artillery wheels at 8½", with plated hub caps. Brilliant
           enamel finish, red frame, blue seat, yellow wheels
1960   Chrome-plated headlights and tank ends.

Cyclops Tractor—(3–6 yrs)

1955   This was renamed, (see under **Minor Tractor** for details).

Flivver—(3–8 yrs)

1954–56   Crank drive; length 33½", width 19". Weight 18 lb; backbone
           is 1½" diameter cycle tubing for strength. Other parts are
           heavy gauge steel. Features a pressed steel seat and rubber
           handgrips; 8½" disc wheels with ⅝" rubber tyres. Large
           nickel-plated hub caps. Enamelled red, wheels white.

Highway Constructor—(2–5 yrs)

1967   Length 34", height 18". Weight 14 lb; 8" disc wheels
           with rubber tyres. Frame made of tubular steel, with
           pressed steel tipping bin, operated from driver's seat
           Adjustable leg room. Enamelled red, with yellow wheels
1968–71   Wheels measured 7". Price: $20.95.

'Pegasus Trotting Gig '

1959–60   Pedal drive; length 40", width 20½". Weight 27½ lb; height
           29". This high-stepping trotting horse, made in pressed
           steel, 'trots' realistically when propelled by the pedals.
           Nylon bearing rear axle, tubular steel frame, comfortable
           saddle and reins for steering.

Harvester Tractor—(3–5 yrs)

1964–65   Crank drive (adjustable); length 28", width 18". Weight 15 lb; moulded one piece 'steel-strong' plastic body, with dual front wheels. Finished in red, yellow, black.

1967–68   Balloon tractor rear wheels, mudguards, large tractor seat.

Junior Farmer Tractor—(3–5 yrs)

1963–64   Front wheel drive; length 28", width 18". Weight 12 lb; moulded in one piece, 'steel-strong' plastic body, super detailed. Features a tractor type seat and mudguards. Front wheels 7", rear 12". Finished in red, yellow, black.

Mighty Tractor—(5–9 yrs)

1963–68   Crank drive (adjustable); length 37", width 25". Weight 36 lb; the 'steel-strong' plastic body is mounted on a sturdy tubular steel frame. Features mudguards, a spring-mounted seat, gear lever and towing hook. Front wheels 10", rear 15". A detailed model of a farm tractor. Finished in red and yellow.

MOTORCYCLES AND MOTOR SCOOTERS POST-1950

Cyclops Jet Motorcycle—(3–5 yrs)

1956   Chain drive; 12" diameter tangent spoke wheels with $^7/_8$" cushion tyres. Weight 14 lb; cycle tubing fork and handlebar with moulded rubber grips. Pressed steel rear fork and frame with integral petrol tank. Dummy engine and large, comfortable saddle. Solid rubber trainer wheels, with rubber pedals, headlight and red rear reflector. Front fork, wheels and saddle enamelled red. Body blue, headlight white. Price: £8 7s 3d ($16.72).

1957   Frame blue; front forks, saddle and wheel rims red.

Cyclops Jet Police Patrol—(3–5 yrs)

1959   Chain drive; 12" cycle spoke wheels. Weight 14 lb; cycle tube handlebars and front forks, pressed steel rear fork and frame with integral petrol tank and dummy engine. Large, comfortable saddle with red rear reflector, horn and aerial. Two-wheel stabiliser on rear wheel, rubber pedals and handgrips and a dummy headlamp. Frame enamelled black, front forks black, saddle and wheel rims yellow.

'Trietta' Pedal Scooter—(5–8 yrs)

1959–61   Chain drive (adjustable for tension); length 40", 12½" diameter pneumatic tyres. Weight 31 lb; heavy-gauge pressed steel unit frame and mudguards. Comfortable saddle, chrome handlebars with clear plastic windshield. Ball bearing hubs, cycle spoke wheels and plated rims. Efficient foot brake operating on rear wheel. Headlight, gleaming red enamel finish. Deluxe replica of Motor Scooter; (see under **Motor Scooter**).

PLASTIC MOULDED MOTORCYCLES and MOTOR SCOOTERS

Junior Motor Bike—(3–5 yrs)
1963   Length 29"; 8" diameter front wheel and 6" diameter rear.
            Weight 12 lb; detailed one piece body of moulded 'steel
            strong' plastic. Features mudguard and twin tube front fork.
            Rear wheels spaced widely for stability; plastic handgrips,
            muffs and streamers. Finished in red.

Junior Motor Scooter—(3–5 yrs)
1963–64   Chain drive (adjustable); length 30" and 10" diameter
            wheels. Weight 18 lb. Completely enclosed, detachable
            trainer wheels. 'Steel strong' moulded plastic body.
            Plastic handgrips, muffs and streamers. Tubular handlebar,
            front mudguard, tail-light and number plate. Finished in red.

'Mustang'—(4–7 yrs)
1967   Length 33"; 12" artillery wheels. Highly detailed 'steel
            strong' moulded plastic body with twin tube handle bars,
            rubber pedals, a front mudguard and removable trainer
            wheels. Natural plastic finish.

'T. T.' Motor Bike—(4–7 yrs)
1963–65   Length 33"; 12" diameter wheels with $^7/_8$" rubber tyres.
            Weight 22 lb; realistic moulded body of 'steel strong'
            plastic that will not chip or dent. Chrome-plated crash bar
            and handlebar; detachable trainer wheels. Front mudguard,
            plastic saddle, pillion seat and plastic 'skid lid'.

DOLLS PRAMS, FOLDERS, STROLLETTES & STROLLERS POST-1950

'Annette' DeLuxe Doll's Folder
1960–61   Body 24"; 7½" wheels with ¾" tyres. Weight 17½ lb;
            shackle suspension, chrome-plated mudguards, tubular
            steel handle, white plastic handgrip. 'Dollyview'
            stormcover, mattress, pillow. Leathercloth body
            to tone with mauve-grey frame and wheels.

'Caprice'
1976   Length 22"; printed vinyl covers and tubular undercarriage.
            All metal body, elegant moulded wheels and folding hood.

'Caress'
1971/72   Length 26"; weight 16 lb. Embossed lift out body, folding
            hood and stormcover.
1976   Length 22"; with 6¾" wheels. Lift out fabric body with
            decorative side panels. Chromed folding undercarriage—
            sturdy, yet elegant.

Doll Crib 20

1968   Length 24"; 6" wheels and moulded tyres. Weight 5 lb; white enamel finish, steel frame, exclusive PVC body, two-tone hood and stormcover. Lift out body for use as a car bed; folds flat for storage .

'Debutante' Doll's Pram DeLuxe

1960   Length 20"; 6½" wheels, ⅝" tyres. Weight 11 lb; plated steel handle, washable plastic handgrip, two-tone plastic hood and stormcover and plated hub caps. Enamelled in gloss colours.

1961   Weight 15 lb; coil spring suspension, chrome-plated mudguards, chrome-plated tubular handle and white plastic handgrip. Wheels 8" in diameter, with ¾" tyres.

1963   Metal body 22" long; body enamelled pastel shades, hood and stormcover to match. Weight 21 lb; wheels and undercarriage white.

1964–65   Referred to as 'Debutante Doll's Pram'.

'Fanfare'

1967   Weight 24 lb; chromed steel door tubes on each side, chromed hub caps and washable lining of pure white plastic. Luxury version of Fantasy; (see under **Fantasy**).

'Fantasy'

1967   Steel body length 22"; 8" wheels, with white cushion tyres. Weight 21 lb; chromed tubular handle, folding hood, and removable stormcover. Body white, with rose transfers. Hood and stormcover in pastel shades.

'Fiesta'

1967   Steel body length 16"; moulded tyres. Weight 4½ lb; white enamel body, blue wheels, and a folding hood.

Doll's Folder 16

1959–64   Length 16"; 3" diameter wheels and ⅜" tyres. Weight 4 lb; leathercloth body, strong steel frame with easy folding action. Folding hood; frame and wheels grey, with leathercloth body to tone.

Doll Folder 18

1967–71   Length 18"; sturdy steel frame. Weight 6 lb; frame and wheels in white enamel. Easy folding action, comes with fold down hood, stormcover and printed fabric covers.

1976   Moulded wheels.

Doll's Folder 20

1963–65   Length 22"; 6" wheels and ½" moulded rubber tyres. Weight 11 lb; embossed leathercloth body, sturdy steel frame, chrome-plated tubular handle and easy folding action. Frame and wheels white.

1970/71   Length 20"; 6½" wheels.

Doll's Folder 20B

1956–57   Length 20", width 9¾" and depth 6"; 5½" pressed steel
           spoke wheels with ³/₈" rubber tyres. Steel constructed
           frame, easy folding action. Nickel-plated hub caps.
           Frame and wheels enamelled cream. Leathercloth covering
           in attractive colours to tone.
1959–60   Frame and wheels enamelled white, with embossed
           leathercloth covering.

Doll Folder 22

1967–71   Length 22"; wheels 6". Weight 11 lb; frame and
           wheels white, PVC body, steel frame with easy
           folding action.

Doll's Folder 24

1959–61   Length 24"; 7" wheels, ⁵/₈" tyres. Weight 17½ lb;
           leathercloth body, sturdy steel frame, tubular handle and
           folding hood with chrome-plated stays. Stormcover, mattress
           and pillow are included. Leathercloth body to tone with
           mauve-grey frame and wheels.
1963–68   No mattress or pillow. Frame and wheels in white.

Doll's Folder 24B

1956   Length 24", width 11" and depth 8"; 7½" wheels with ⁵/₈"
           rubber tyres. Steel constructed frame with easy folding
           action. Adjustable drop end, best quality lined
           leathercloth. Folding hood with leathercloth cover to
           match body, unlined. Nickel-plated hood stays.
           Leathercloth stormcover to match. Nickel-plated tubular
           handle. One piece pressed steel nickel-plated mudguards.
           Nickel-plated hub caps. Frame and wheels enamelled in
           attractive colours. Upholstery to tone.
1957   Stormcover added.

Doll's Folder 24B DeLuxe

1959   Length 24"; 7½" wheels, ¾" tyres. Weight 17½ lb;
           features shackle suspension, chrome-plated mudguards
           and tubular steel handle, with white plastic handgrip.
           'Dolly-View' stormcover; mattress and pillow included.
           Leathercloth body to tone with mauve-grey frame and
           wheels.

Junior Airline

1963–68   Weight 23 lb; 7½" wheels, ¾" white cushion tyres.
           Replica of Baby Carriage. Finely woven lift out cane body
           for conversion to doll cot or bassinette. Chrome-plated
           handle, hood stays, mudguards and tubular surround rail.
           'Dolly view' stormcover, coil spring suspension, folding
           handle and embossed leathercloth hood. Body enamelled
           in white.

Junior 'Ballerina'

1964–65   Weight 24 lb; 7½" wheels, ¾" white cushion tyres. Styled
           after Baby Carriage. Welded steel body, upholstered
           throughout with washable white lining. Lift out body
           for conversion to doll bassinette or cot. Chrome-plated
           handle, mudguards, tubular surround rail. Folding hood,
           coil spring suspension, and vinyl covers.

Junior 'Lift Out' 370 Doll's Pram

1959 Length 26"; 7½" wheels and ¾" tyres. Weight 23 lb; replica of Cyclops 370 Baby Carriage. Twin tube lifting bars, chrome-plated mudguards and wheels, chrome-plated handle with white plastic grip, spring suspension, 'lift out' body for conversion to bassinette or cot, 'Dolly View' stormcover, folding handle and hood. Leathercloth body in a variety of colours.

1960–61 'Fleur' pattern leathercloth.

1963 Renamed 'Junior 370'; weight 22 lb.

'Madeira' Doll's Pram

1961 Length 22"; 8" diameter wheels, ¾" tyres. Weight 18 lb; welded steel body, upholstered throughout with washable white plastic. Chrome-plated tubular handle and hub caps, plastic grip and coil spring suspension. Body and undergear white to blend with two-tone blue-grey fabric combination on hood and stormcover.

'Majorca'

1961 Contemporary-style doll carriage with samebasic specifications as Madeira. Has additional chrome-plated tubular side rails and mudguards.

1963–65 Weight 20 lb; two tone fabric combination on hood and stormcover.

Doll's Pram

1950–51 Length 20"; all metal, with rubber tyred wheels and folding hood. Price: £3 17s 6d ($7.75).

Doll's Pram No. 1

1953 Length 19"; 6" wheels with rubber tyres. Also comes with folding hood. Price: £5 10s ($11.00).

Doll's Pram No. 16

1956 Length 16"; 5½" pressed steel spoke wheels, ³/₈" rubber tyres. Body in best sheet steel with distinctive moulding. Washable plastic folding hood in colour to tone with body panel. Sturdy round steel handle. Body enamelled blue, with handle and undergear in white.

1957 Stormcover added.

1959 Body enamelled pink with blue decorative trim.

1960–68 Body and undergear white with red decorative trim; wheels in white. Price: $11.95.

1970–76 Printed hood and stormcover; wheels 6".

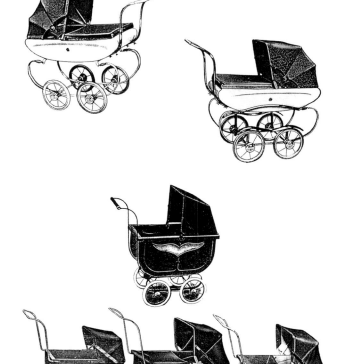

Doll's Pram No. 20

1955 Length 20"; metal body with washable folding hood. Rubber tyred wheels. Price: £5 ($10.00).

1956–59 Weight 11 lb; 6½" wheels, ⁵/₈" rubber tyres. Washable plastic folding hood in colour to tone with body panel and washable plastic stormcover to match. Nickel-plated hub caps. Body, undergear and handle enamelled in cream. Hood and stormcover in contrasting colours to tone.

1960–65 Enamelled in gloss colours.

1968 Body and wheels white.

1971/72 Printed hood and stormcover.

Doll's Pram No. 24

1956–57   Length 24"; 8" wheels with $^{7}/_{16}$" rubber tyres. Body of best quality sheet steel with distinctive mouldings. Folding hood, with leathercloth cover. Nickel-plated stays, leathercloth stormcover and folding tubular nickel-plated handle. Nickel-plated hub caps; body enamelled primrose, lined blue, with rose transfer. Undergear and wheels silver.

1959–60   Body enamelled in pastel colours, undercarriage and wheels in white. Shackle suspension and $^{5}/_{8}$" rubber tyres.

'Robin'

1971/72   Length 19"; 6½" wheels. Metal, convex shaped body, brilliant hood and stormcover.

'Sparrow' Doll's Pram

1963–64   Weight 5 lb; wheels 6" with ½" moulded rubber tyres. Features contour-formed metal body with attached hood and stormcover. Chrome-plated handle and plastic handgrip. Attractive enamel finish, contrasting hood and stormcover.

Stroller Crib 5

1967   Length 24"; 6" wheels, moulded tyres. Weight 5 lb; sturdy steel frame and white enamel finish. PVC body, two-tone hood and stormcover. Lift out body for use as a car bed. Folds flat for storage.

Stroller Crib 6

1967   Length 24". Weight 7 lb; enlarged version of Stroller Crib 5.

'Tina'

1976   Length 17"; stylish metal body and sturdy frame. Folding hood in printed vinyl. White moulded wheels.

Toddle Stroller

1970/71   Length 13"; 5" diameter wide track wheels. Weight 6 lb; lift out body mounted on tubular steel chassis. Tubular handle, folding hood and stormcover.

STROLLERS

'Brolly'

1976   Folding umbrella style that is all the rage, in modern denim print. Small double moulded twin wheels. Just like Mum!

'Dianne' Doll's Chariot with Hood.

1960–65   Same as the Juliet, but with the addition of a folding built in hood of matching PVC; (see under **Juliet**).

1967–71   Weight 6 lb; Same look as Juliet, but with detachable hood and shopping bag of matching PVC; (see under **Juliet**).

1971/72   Height 27".

1976   Moulded wheels.

'Juliet' Doll's Chariot

1960–65	Height 28"; 5½" diameter new style pressed steel wheels with moulded tyres. Weight 5 lb; light steel frame that folds in one movement to compact size. Cover bright P.V.C. with white washable lining. Frame and wheels white.
1967–71	Wheels 6".
1971/72	Height 27".

'Marie' Doll's Chariot DeLuxe

1960–61	Weight 5 lb; 5½" wheels with moulded rubber tyres. Luxury doll's stroller with adjustable backrest and footrest. 'Monaco' pattern PVC cover, washable line, chrome-plated tubular handle and plastic grip.
1953	Height 22"; folds into compact size. Price: £2 3s ($4.30).
1955	Doll's stroller, folds completely. Disc wheels, tyred. Price £1 17s 6d ($3.75).
1956	Height 23"; light steel frame that folds in one movement to compact size. Rubber tyred steel disc wheels. Enamelled in bright colours; canvas seat to tone.

Nibs Chariot No. 2

1955	With headrest and spoked wheels (no canopy). Price: £3 3s 6d ($6.35). With canopy: price: £3 13s 6d ($7.35).
1956–57	Height 26"; 5½" wheels, $^{7}/_{16}$" rubber tyres. Light steel frame, folds in one movement to compact size. Nickel-plated hub caps. Frame and wheels enamelled in bright colours. Canvas seat to tone.
1959	White plastic handgrip and guard rail. Plastic play rings. Covered in strong tartan cloth; frame in red, with white wheels.

Doll's Nibs Chariot 2H.

1956–57	Same as No. 2, with the addition of a folding hood; (see under **Nibs Chariot No. 2**).
1959	Same as No. 2, but with a contemporary hood in matching tartan; (see under **Nibs Chariot No. 2**).

Nibs 3 DeLuxe

1959	Weight 5 lb; 5½" wheels, with moulded rubber tyres. Adjustable backrest and footrest. Gay 'Monaco' PVC cover with washable lining, chrome-plated tubular handle with plastic grip.

Nibs Twinette

1959	Height 26"; 5½" wheels, with moulded rubber tyres. Weight 7¼ lb; strong steel frame, with easy folding action. Individual compartments for each doll, gay tartan canvas cover, built in folding hood, and a white plastic handgrip. Blue frame, and white wheels.
1960–61	Gay colourful cover; blue frame, and white wheels.
1963	Wheels 6"; hood has a fringe. Frame and wheels in white.

'Polyanna'

1971/72	Height 30"; pre-painted rolled steel frame and exclusive washable cover, detachable hood and shopping bag. Weight 3 lb.

'Sunkar'

1967–71	Height 22½"; wheels 6". Weight 5 lbs; chromed tubular steel frame and handle, ultra-modern styling, white enamel, rubber tyres, and easy folding action.

'Susan' Doll's Chariot DeLuxe with Hood

1960–61   Identical in design to Marie Doll's Chariot, with
          additional built in folding hood and shopping bag. Gay
          PVC colours with white lining; (see under **Marie Doll's
          Chariot**).
1963   Weight 6 lb; 6" wheels, moulded rubber tyres. Features
          large capacity shopping bag and detachable hood
          plus an adjustable back rest. Chrome-plated tubular
          handle with plastic grip. Gaily coloured PVC cover with
          washable nursery lining.
1964–65   Weight 7 lb; bobble-fringed hood, fully enclosed side
          curtains, and a shopping bag combined with rear curtain.

DOLL'S STROLLETTES

1950–51   With steel folding frame and rubber tyred wheels.
1951–52   With flat steel frame and rubber tyred wheels.
          Price: (for DeLuxe version) £5 5s ($10.50).

'Teena'

1967–72   Weight 7 lb; wheels 6". Bobble-fringed hood. Fully
          enclosed side curtains, shopping bag, adjustable
          backrest.

Toddler Doll's Chariot

1960–61   Height 23"; rubber tyred steel disc wheels. Weight 3½ lb;
          light steel frame that folds in one movement to compact
          size. Enamelled white frame, with gay PVC cover
          and lining.
1963–65   Nursery print lining.
1967–72   Exclusive PVC cover.
1976   Metal footrest.

'Wendy' Doll's Chariot

1961–72   Weight 4 lb. As basic specification for 'Toddler' with
          addition of detachable hood and shopping bag in
          matching fabric.
1976   Moulded wheels.

PLASTIC MOULDED PRAMS

'Anne'

1968–76   Length 16"; 6" plastic wheels. Weight 4 lb; moulded plastic
          body set on sturdy steel chassis, with adjustable hood in
          PVC fabric, plated steel handle. Price: $8.75.

'Countess'

1968   Length 18"; 6" wheels with contrasting colour tyres.
          Weight 4 lb; replica of full-size pram— stylish body
          mounted on round springs. PVC hood cover.
          Price: $13.95.

'Duchess'

1970–72   Length 22"; 6" wheels. Weight 12 lb; lift out body with
          embossed panels on a steel frame, tubular handle,
          vacuum-plated, easy folding action.

'Linnet'

1968–70/71 Length 20"; 6" wheels with contrasting colour tyres. Weight 6 lb; one piece moulded body, with PVC two-tone hood and tubular steel chassis with coil spring suspension and a plated tubular steel handle. Price: $14.95–$16.50.

'Princess'

1968–70/71 Length 24"; 7" wheels. Weight 7½ lb; moulded one piece plastic body. Tubular chassis with coil spring suspension, chrome-plated tubular handle, and PVC hood and stormcover. Price: $20.50.

1971/72 Vacuum metallicised 7" wheels.

'Polyanne' Doll Pram

1963–65 Length 14"; 5" diameter wheels. Weight 2½ lb; moulded plastic body, sturdy steel undercarriage and plated steel handle. Folding hood in attractive colour to tone with body. Natural finish in blue and yellow.

Cyclops
MOTOR CARS

SUPER SPORTS

BEETLE: 1975–76

ARMY JEEP: 1984–85

BEACH BUGGY: 1970–71
BEACH BUGGY (Electric): 1970–71

BEACH BUGGY: 1971–72
BEACH BUGGY (Electric): 1971–72

FIRE KAR: 1988

C.D. GO-KART
1988

GO-KART
1976

FERRARI: 1984–85

FORMULA 3
1976

FLYER CAR

FORMULA 2
1975

G.T. SPORTS DELUXE
1975

G.T. SPORTS DELUXE
1976

G.T. SPORTS: 1968–75
(1972 Version)

MOON BUG: 1970–71

HI-WAY PATROL: 1976

LE MANS: 1984–85

HAPPY CART: 1984

OFF ROAD JEEP: 1984

OFF ROADER: 1988

ROW CAR: 1984

SCAMP: 1968

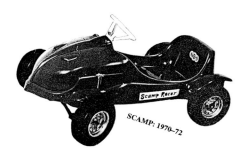

SCAMP: 1970–72

SCAMP DELUXE: 1970–71

SKAT KART: 1970–76

SPACE BUG: 1971–72

SPACE CRUISER: 1984–88

SPORTS CAR: 1962

JUNIOR GALAXY BUSTER
1988

JUNIOR MOON MISS
1988

Cyclops

JUNIOR TANDEM
1963–64

JUNIOR TANDEM GIRLS
1988

JUNIOR TANDEM
1967

JUNIOR
TANDEM BOYS
1988

LI'L MISS
TRIKE: 1984

MITE-Y TRIKE
1984

MX TRIKE: 1984

PIRATE BIN TRICYCLE
1963

PIRATE BIN
TRICYCLE: 1964

POLICE TRIKE
1984

RAINBOW
TRIKE: 1984

1988
RAINBOW TRIKE

SENIOR
TANDEM TRIKE
1967

SENIOR TANDEM
TRIKE: 1976

SENIOR TANDEM
TRIKE: 1988

SENIOR TANDEM TRIKE
1963–65

SIREN TRIKE
1964–65

SUPER
16 TRIKE–1967
20 TRIKE–1967

SUPER TRIKE
1967

SHUTTLE
TRIKE: 1984

TRIKES

SUPER TANDEM
1976

THUNDEROD
1965

TANDEM TRIKE: 1959

SIREN TRIKE: 1967

CHAIN-DRIVE TRICYCLE 112: 1956–57

CHAIN-DRIVE TRICYCLE 116 1963–65

CHAIN-DRIVE TRICYCLE 112 With bin: 1957

CHAIN-DRIVE TRICYCLE 116 1956–57

CHAIN-DRIVE TRICYCLE 116: 1967

CHAIN-DRIVE TRICYCLE 117 1959–61

CHAIN DRIVE TRICYCLE 117: 1967

CHAIN-DRIVE TRICYCLE 117 1963–65

TRICYCLE 212: 1950–60

CHAIN-DRIVE TRICYCLE SUPER 117 1967

TRICYCLE 212: 1967

TRICYCLE 212B: 1967

TRICYCLE 212 1961–65

TRICYCLE 216B 1956–59

TRICYCLE 216 1960

TRICYCLE 216B: 1961–65

TRICYCLE 216B: 1967

TRICYCLE 220: 1956–63

TRICYCLE 310: 1956–57

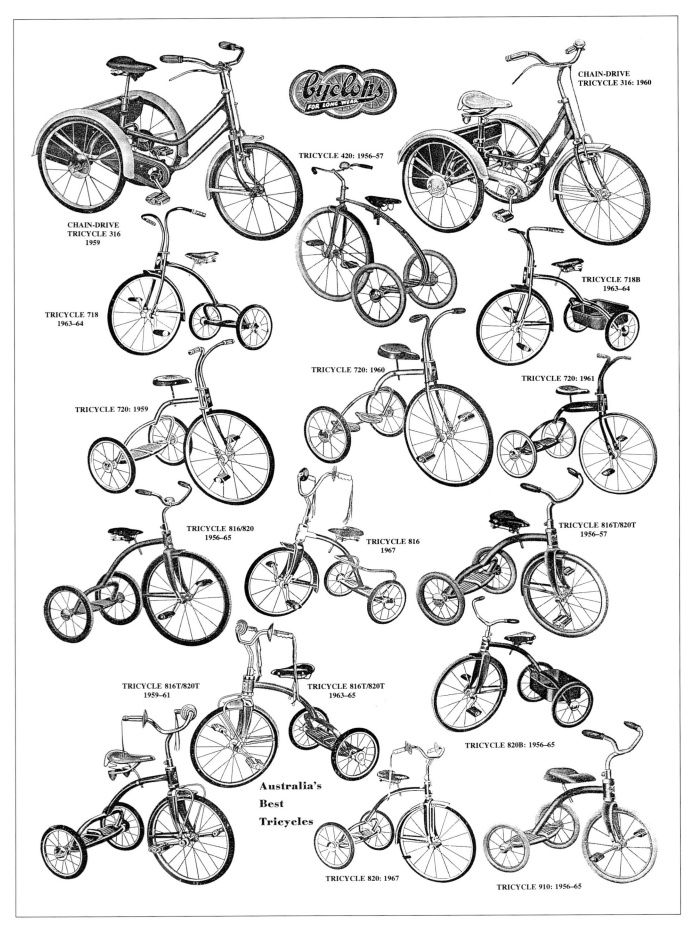

CHAIN-DRIVE
TRICYCLE 316: 1960

TRICYCLE 420: 1956–57

CHAIN-DRIVE
TRICYCLE 316
1959

TRICYCLE 718
1963–64

TRICYCLE 718B
1963–64

TRICYCLE 720: 1959

TRICYCLE 720: 1960

TRICYCLE 720: 1961

TRICYCLE 816/820
1956–65

TRICYCLE 816
1967

TRICYCLE 816T/820T
1956–57

TRICYCLE 816T/820T
1959–61

TRICYCLE 816T/820T
1963–65

TRICYCLE 820B: 1956–65

Australia's
Best
Tricycles

TRICYCLE 820: 1967

TRICYCLE 910: 1956–65

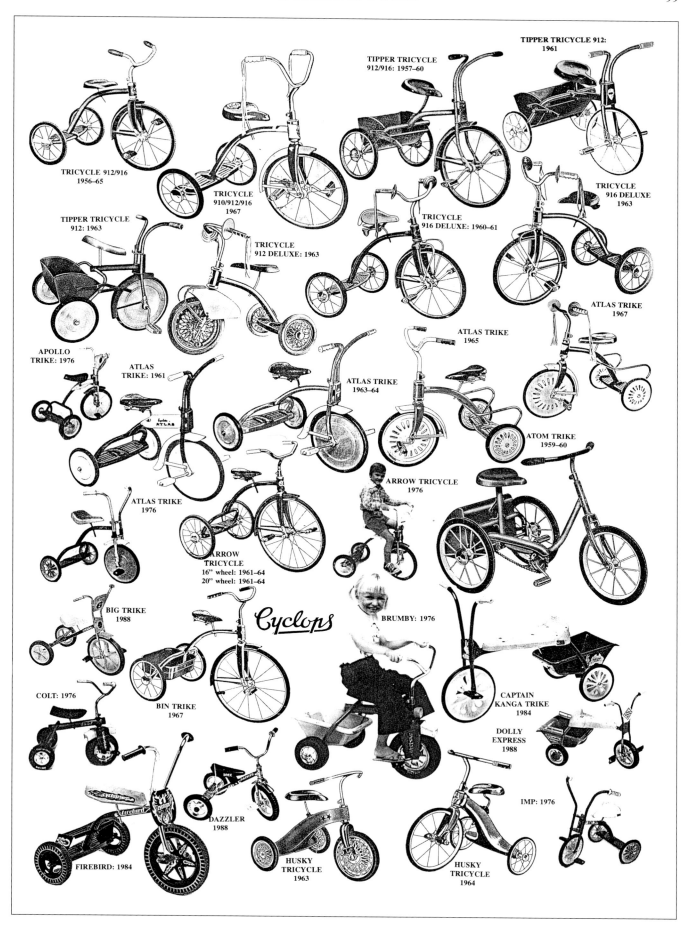

TIPPER TRICYCLE 912: 1961

TIPPER TRICYCLE 912/916: 1957–60

TRICYCLE 912/916 1956–65

TRICYCLE 910/912/916 1967

TRICYCLE 916 DELUXE 1963

TIPPER TRICYCLE 912: 1963

TRICYCLE 912 DELUXE: 1963

TRICYCLE 916 DELUXE: 1960–61

ATLAS TRIKE 1967

APOLLO TRIKE: 1976

ATLAS TRIKE: 1961

ATLAS TRIKE 1963–64

ATLAS TRIKE 1965

ATOM TRIKE 1959–60

ATLAS TRIKE 1976

ARROW TRICYCLE 16" wheel: 1961–64 20" wheel: 1961–64

ARROW TRICYCLE 1976

BIG TRIKE 1988

Cyclops

BRUMBY: 1976

CAPTAIN KANGA TRIKE 1984

COLT: 1976

BIN TRIKE 1967

DOLLY EXPRESS 1988

IMP: 1976

FIREBIRD: 1984

DAZZLER 1988

HUSKY TRICYCLE 1963

HUSKY TRICYCLE 1964

TANDEM TRIKE: 1960

TAXI TRIKE: 1967

TAXI TIPPER DELUXE: 1976

TAXI TIPPER DELUXE 1984

TIPPER TRIKE 1967

TIPPER TRIKE: 1976

CYCLOBIKE 514 1956–57

SUPER 16 BIKE 1960

PEDAL PUSHER: 1963–65 JUNIOR PEDAL PUSHER: 1967

COMMANDO CYCLE: 1959

Cyclops FOR LONG WEAR

FOLDABYKE 1967

MARVEL 1967

FAIRY CYCLE 516T 1957–59 CYCLE 516T: 1960

BICYCLES

SENIOR PEDAL PUSHER 1967

TIGER BIKE: 1967

PIRATE BIKE: 1967

BANDIT BIKE: 1967

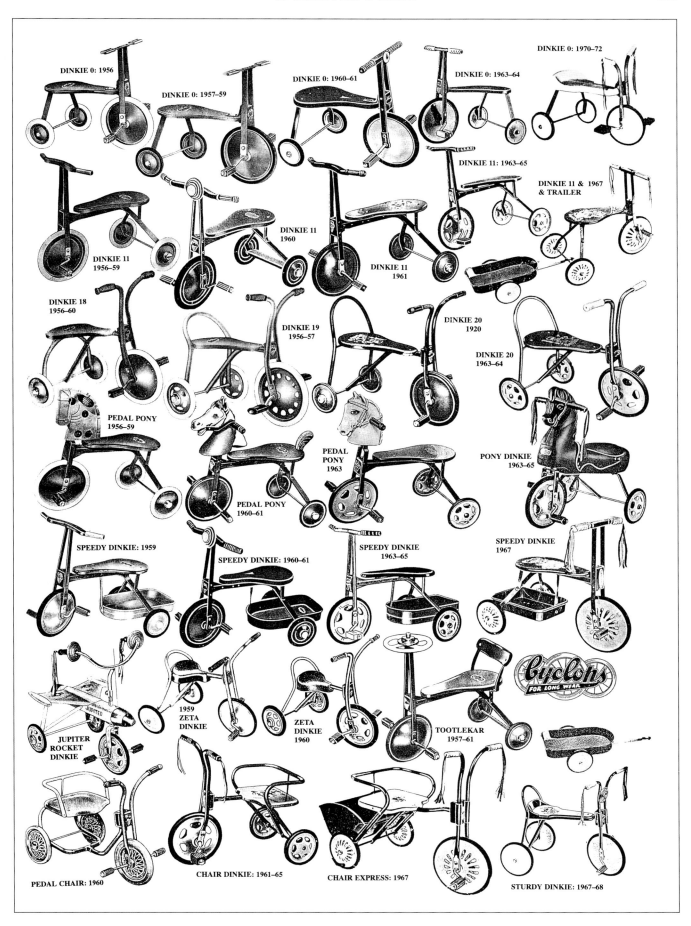

DINKIE 0: 1956

DINKIE 0: 1957–59

DINKIE 0: 1960–61

DINKIE 0: 1963–64

DINKIE 0: 1970–72

DINKIE 11: 1963–65

DINKIE 11 & 1967 & TRAILER

DINKIE 11 1956–59

DINKIE 11 1960

DINKIE 11 1961

DINKIE 18 1956–60

DINKIE 19 1956–57

DINKIE 20 1920

DINKIE 20 1963–64

PEDAL PONY 1956–59

PEDAL PONY 1960–61

PEDAL PONY 1963

PONY DINKIE 1963–65

SPEEDY DINKIE: 1959

SPEEDY DINKIE: 1960–61

SPEEDY DINKIE 1963–65

SPEEDY DINKIE 1967

JUPITER ROCKET DINKIE

1959 ZETA DINKIE

ZETA DINKIE 1960

TOOTLEKAR 1957–61

Cyclops FOR LONG WEAR

PEDAL CHAIR: 1960

CHAIR DINKIE: 1961–65

CHAIR EXPRESS: 1967

STURDY DINKIE: 1967–68

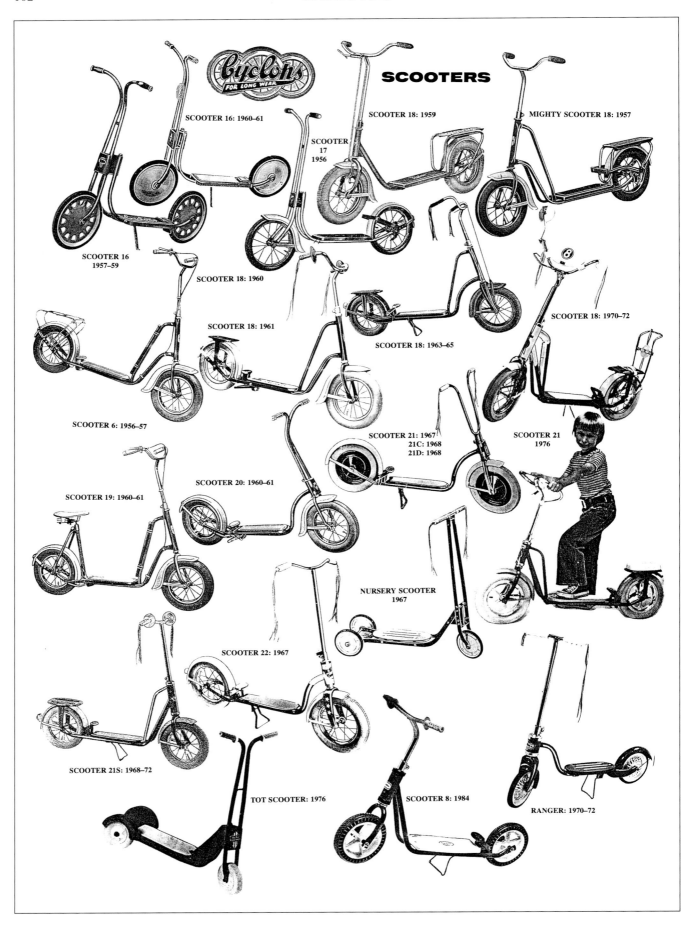

SCOOTER 16: 1960–61

SCOOTERS

SCOOTER 18: 1959

MIGHTY SCOOTER 18: 1957

SCOOTER 17 1956

SCOOTER 16 1957–59

SCOOTER 18: 1960

SCOOTER 18: 1970–72

SCOOTER 18: 1961

SCOOTER 18: 1963–65

SCOOTER 6: 1956–57

SCOOTER 21: 1967 21C: 1968 21D: 1968

SCOOTER 21 1976

SCOOTER 19: 1960–61

SCOOTER 20: 1960–61

NURSERY SCOOTER 1967

SCOOTER 22: 1967

SCOOTER 21S: 1968–72

TOT SCOOTER: 1976

SCOOTER 8: 1984

RANGER: 1970–72

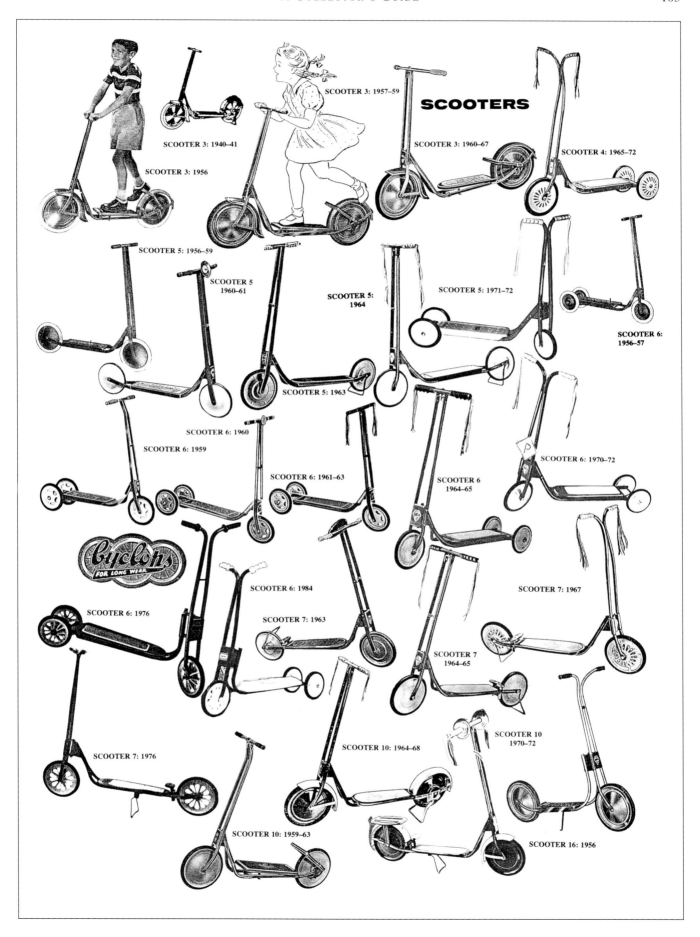

SCOOTER 3: 1940–41

SCOOTER 3: 1956

SCOOTER 3: 1957–59

SCOOTERS

SCOOTER 3: 1960–67

SCOOTER 4: 1965–72

SCOOTER 5: 1956–59

SCOOTER 5
1960–61

SCOOTER 5:
1964

SCOOTER 5: 1971–72

SCOOTER 6:
1956–57

SCOOTER 5: 1963

SCOOTER 6: 1960

SCOOTER 6: 1959

SCOOTER 6: 1961–63

SCOOTER 6
1964–65

SCOOTER 6: 1970–72

SCOOTER 6: 1984

SCOOTER 7: 1967

SCOOTER 6: 1976

SCOOTER 7: 1963

SCOOTER 7
1964–65

SCOOTER 7: 1976

SCOOTER 10: 1964–68

SCOOTER 10
1970–72

SCOOTER 10: 1959–63

SCOOTER 16: 1956

ROCKERS

AERO ROCKER
1959

AERO ROCKER
1960–61

BEAUTY ROCKER: 1976

CAR CAR ROCKER
1957–63

CAR CAR
ROCKER: 1964

CAR CAR ROCKER
1967–68

CAR CAR
ROCKER

CAR CAR ROCKER
1976–84

CIRCUS ROCKER
1971–72

CIRCUS ROCKER
BOUNCER: 1971–72

CONVERTIBLE ROCKER/TABLE & BENCH: 1985

COWBOY
ROCKER
1963–67

DINKIE
ROCKER
1960

FOXHUNTER ROCKER
1959–61

GEE GEE
ROCKER
1957–59

GEE GEE
ROCKER
1963

GEE GEE
ROCKER: 1971–72

GEE GEE
ROCKER
1960–61

GEE GEE
ROCKER
1964–67

KANGAROO
ROCKER: 1986–87

GEE GEE
ROCKER
1976–87

JUMPING JUMBO: 1967–71

JUNIOR
ROCKING HORSE: 1967–68

MOTOR ROCKER: 1963

MOTOR ROCKER
1964

MIDNIGHT
ROCKER
1971–72

MIDNIGHT ROCKER: 1976

MOTOR ROCKER: 1967

ROCKERS

MUSTANG ROCKER: 1963

NURSERY ROCKER
1956–59

PLUSH PONY ROCKER
1967–68

PONY ROCKER: 1963

Cyclops
FOR LONG WEAR.

PRANCING PONY
1957–61

PRANCING PONY: 1963
PRANCING PONY JUNIOR: 1964–67

PRANCING PONY SENIOR
1964–67

SENIOR PRANCING
PONY: 1968
PRANCING PONY: 1970–72

ROCKING HORSE: 1970

ROCKING HORSE: 1976

ROCK'N'ROLL: 1960

SENIOR ROCKING HORSE: 1967

SHOO FLY ROCKER: 1967

TWIN ROCKER
1967–68
TANDEM ROCKER: 1970–71

WEE ROCKER: 1968

WOODEN ROCKING HORSE: 1984–87

TIP LORRY: 1957–60

CYCLOPS DIESEL
DELIVERY VAN: 1957–61

CYCLOPS SUPER DIESEL SERIES

CYCLOPS DIESEL FARM TRUCK: 1957–60

CYCLOPS DIESEL SHELL TANKER: 1957–60

CYCLOPS DIESEL CRASH WAGGON: 1959

CYCLOPS DIESEL FIRE ENGINE: 1959

CYCLOPS DIESEL FRONT LOADER: 1959–60

*300 SERIES
PULL-A-LONG*

CYCLOPS DOCKSIDE CRANE: 1957–59

CYCLOPS DELIVERY VAN 302
1957–64

CYCLOPS FLASHER TRUCK 301: 1957–61

CYCLOPS DIESEL FLASHER: 1963–64

CYCLOPS SHELL WAGGON 304: 1957–61

CYCLOPS TIP LORRY 303: 1957–64

CYCLOPS 400 SERIES

CYCLOPS TIPPER TRUCK 401: 1960

CYCLOPS TRANSPORT VAN 400: 1960–61

CYCLOPS LOW LOADER TRANSPORTER: 1963–64

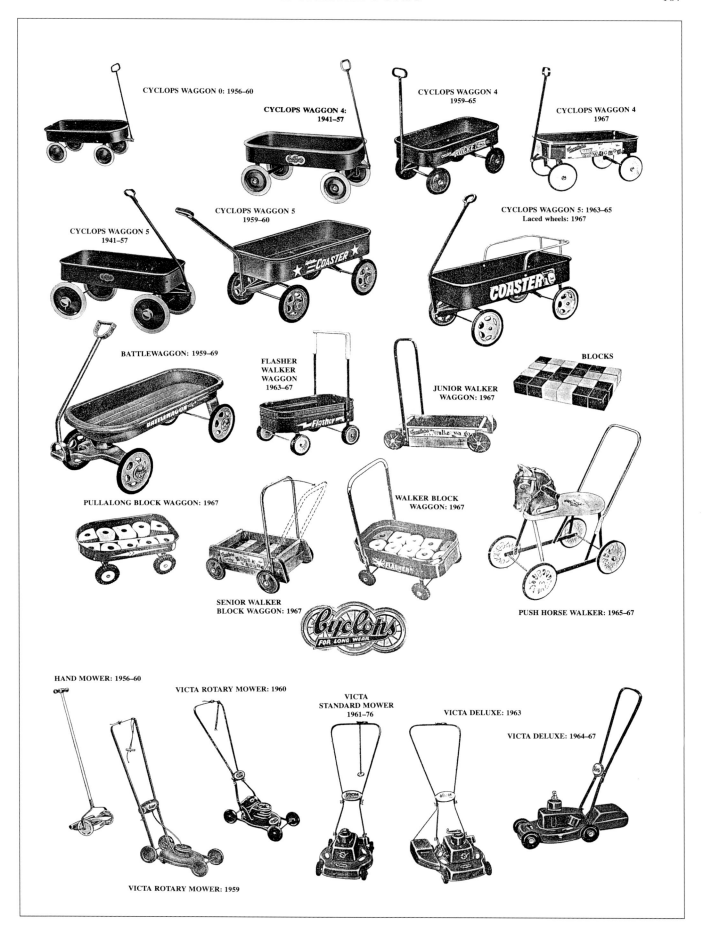

CYCLOPS WAGGON 0: 1956–60

CYCLOPS WAGGON 4:
1941–57

CYCLOPS WAGGON 4
1959–65

CYCLOPS WAGGON 4
1967

CYCLOPS WAGGON 5
1941–57

CYCLOPS WAGGON 5
1959–60

CYCLOPS WAGGON 5: 1963–65
Laced wheels: 1967

BATTLEWAGGON: 1959–69

FLASHER
WALKER
WAGGON
1963–67

JUNIOR WALKER
WAGGON: 1967

BLOCKS

PULLALONG BLOCK WAGGON: 1967

WALKER BLOCK
WAGGON: 1967

SENIOR WALKER
BLOCK WAGGON: 1967

PUSH HORSE WALKER: 1965–67

HAND MOWER: 1956–60

VICTA ROTARY MOWER: 1960

VICTA
STANDARD MOWER
1961–76

VICTA DELUXE: 1963

VICTA DELUXE: 1964–67

VICTA ROTARY MOWER: 1959

INDEX